futura

THE TYPE OF TODAY
AND TO-MORROW

NEVE
FUT

R USE

URA

NEVER USE
FUTURA

DOUGLAS THOMAS

PRINCETON ARCHITECTURAL PRESS

NEW YORK

PUBLISHED BY
Princeton Architectural Press
A McEvoy Group company
37 East 7th Street, New York, NY 10003
202 Warren Street, Hudson, New York 12534
Visit our website at www.papress.com

© 2017 Douglas Thomas
Foreword © Ellen Lupton, 2017
All rights reserved

Printed and bound in China

20 19 18 17 4 3 2 1 First edition

ISBN 978-1-61689-572-3

No part of this book may be used or reproduced in any manner without written permission from the publisher, except in the context of reviews.

Every reasonable attempt has been made to identify owners of copyright. Errors or omissions will be corrected in subsequent editions.

EDITOR
Barbara Darko

DESIGNER
Douglas Thomas

SPECIAL THANKS TO
Janet Behning, Nolan Boomer, Nicola Brower, Abby Bussel, Tom Cho, Benjamin English, Jenny Florence, Jan Cigliano Hartman, Susan Hershberg, Lia Hunt, Mia Johnson, Valerie Kamen, Simone Kaplan-Senchak, Jennifer Lippert, Kristy Maier, Sara McKay, Eliana Miller, Wes Seeley, Rob Shaeffer, Sara Stemen, Paul Wagner, and Joseph Weston of Princeton Architectural Press
—*Kevin C. Lippert, publisher*

Library of Congress Cataloging-in-Publication Data is available from the publisher upon request.

FOR RUTH

FOREWORD, FUTURA!

Foreword
by Ellen Lupton

12

BACK TO THE FUTURA

Introduction

18

1
MY OTHER MODERNISM IS IN FUTURA

How Futura helped pioneer the advance of modernism

24

2
SPARTAN GEOMETRY

Why you've never truly used Futura unless your name is Erik Spiekermann

46

3
DEGENERATE TYPOGRAPHY

The politics of Futura, from Communists to Conservatives and everyone in between

64

4
OVER THE MOON FOR FUTURA

From post offices to the Mercury program, Futura was the official typeface of the American Century

86

5
FUTURA IN THE WILD

Why David Carson was wrong and Massimo Vignelli was right (again)

104

6
SHOW ME THE MONEY

$10,000 handbags and high-end design

130

NEVER USE FUTURA?

Epilogue

176

7
PAST, PRESENT, FUTURA

On nostalgia and the zeitgeist of contemporary typography

146

Acknowledgments

183

Notes

187

Image Credits

199

Index

201

8
FUTURA BY ANY OTHER NAME

Tailored typefaces and corporate storytelling

162

FOREWORD, FUTURA!

SOME PEOPLE JUST DON'T GET IT. They don't get that every typeface has its own DNA, its own voice, and its own hidden history of intrigue and excess. Some people don't get that you can express your love for something by showing how hopelessly tired and overused it is. This is a book for people who get it. This is a book for type snobs.

Douglas Thomas is the most charming, generous, open-minded type snob I have ever met. Not all type snobs are like that. If you are one and you're reading this book, you are probably not as charming as Doug. Yes, you're an erudite observer of kerning pairs and bracketed serifs. You know the difference between asterisks, asterisms, and asteroids, but you don't know that interrobangs have no place in polite conversation. Doug, on the other hand, knows how to get normal people to think about type. He draws you in with subjects of general interest, such as the hidden links between Nazi politics, Richard Nixon, and the moon landing. (No, it's not a paranoid conspiracy. It's Futura!)

PREVIOUS
Beware of Dog sign, in Futura, in Bolton Hill, Baltimore, 2016

Be warned: a book is a dangerous thing. A young woman approached me after a lecture recently to say that my book *Thinking with Type* was the first book she had ever really understood. I smiled warmly and shook her hand, yet despair clouded my heart. Was it the first book about type she had ever understood, or the first book on any subject? Introduced through the innocuous pages of a college textbook, typography will soon stalk you everywhere. You cease to find solace and sustenance at the supermarket; instead, you puzzle over the diamond-shaped tittles that dot the *i*'s of the Triscuit logo. Passing by an ice-cream shop with a sign set in Papyrus and Comic Sans, you wander inside and order two scoops of dog poop. One day you step off the edge of the subway platform wondering whether the words "STAND BEHIND THE YELLOW LINE" are set in Akzidenz Grotesk or Helvetica.

When you read this book by Doug, matters will get even worse. *Never Use Futura* will immerse you in the fluid mechanics of typographic influence. Once a typeface enters the veins of society, there is no escape. Futura seeped into every corner of modern life by exploiting the forces of technology and commerce, taste and convenience, meaning and metaphor. Futura is a specific historical artifact, authored by the German designer Paul Renner in the 1920s, but it is also an idea, a concept about geometric construction that has inspired mindless clones and copies, as well as original designs infused with their own identity and authorship.

If you are a newcomer to typography, you might glance at the title of this book and wonder, "Isn't there a movie about that?" No! Make no mistake: Futura played a far bigger role in the history of twentieth-century design—and the history of the twentieth century in general—than any other typeface, including one overplayed diva who debuted in Switzerland in 1957. Futura is the most enduring typographic act of its time, shaping the drama of design, advertising, and public communication for decades to come. It remains very much on view today. You'll see live performances every day at the post office, at the mall, and in countless student design projects, where its round *O*s and pointy *M*s and *V*s make it go-to fodder for abstract type compositions and expressive word marks. (Doug discovered that such student projects date back to the 1930s, when aspiring modernists drafted their own variants of Futura in order to master the arts of advertising layout and headline lettering.)

How did Douglas Thomas become such a kind, pleasant, socially well-adjusted type snob? He studied design in the outstanding BFA program at Brigham Young University in Provo, Utah, where he sometimes used Futura. He went on to earn an MA in history at the University of Chicago, where he conducted primary research on the reception of Futura (and Helvetica) in the United States. In Chicago he honed his skills as a historian, spending long hours at the Regenstein and Newberry Libraries exploring obscure trade journals about the midcentury type industry. He earned his MFA in graphic design at Maryland Institute College of Art (MICA), where I was proud to work with him as graduate faculty and an adviser on this project. Doug knew when he arrived at MICA in 2014 that he wanted to write a cultural biography of Futura.

Employing his rigor as a historian and his eye as a designer, he used approachable prose and a lovingly curated collection of visual artifacts to tell fascinating stories about the social life of type.

Behold! Be bold! Be light, narrow, or extra condensed! The thing about type snobs is that the stuff we love is everywhere. You don't need to visit a distant vineyard or an upscale restaurant to delight in the subtleties of counters, bowls, and finials. Typography is right here at the bus station and the big-box store—the muggles just haven't noticed yet. Have no fear of x-heights! The brother- and sisterhood of type snobs welcomes you with our not-so-secret handshake.

—Ellen Lupton, 2017

NET WT.
4 OZ.
(113g)

SWEET (UNSALTED)
BUTTER
PACKED BY PLANT 27-031

GRADE
AA

Almost a century of widespread industrial use means that Futura is everywhere. Just wait—after you read this book, grocery shopping will never be the same.

BACK TO THE FUTURA

WHEN I STARTED DESIGN CLASSES in 2003, my education began (like for many designers before and many since) with simple exercises derived from Bauhaus and Swiss masters. These lessons in typography, composition, and grids included guidance for navigating the thousands of choices available to anyone with a computer and a layout program.[1] My teachers gave me advice about the best typefaces to use and, just as crucially, the ones to avoid. Most of their directives made sense: no free fonts, since they are often imperfectly made and lack basic features like good spacing; boycott Comic Sans, Papyrus, or anything goofy; avoid type by Goudy and Zapf, or anything from ITC (the International Typeface Corporation) to keep your work from looking dated. If you've taught design classes or art directed new designers, you've probably given similar counsel. But there was one piece of advice that was hard for me to understand.

"Never use Futura"? Why would my teachers tell me to avoid one of the most successful and iconic

PREVIOUS
From 1932 to 2005 Crayola crayons used the most ubiquitous typeface of the twentieth century in its packaging and labeling: Futura.

typefaces of the twentieth century? That exhortation seemed bizarre then, and I've heard others repeat it since, even though Futura is commonly introduced as the quintessential geometric sans serif in design books.[2] Futura is used in every American mall and in thousands of advertisements, posters, marquees, and signs across the world. It's easily a moniker of not just modern life but also modernism. Aren't graphic design history books full of projects in Futura? Even new brand identities and book covers by today's design trendsetters use it. How is it that great designers keep turning to Futura, but some tell their students to stay clear of it?

Even though I had chafed at the directive to never use Futura, I caught myself giving the same counsel to my students when I taught my first Type I course at Maryland Institute College of Art in 2014. The prescription remained practical, almost ideological, even after a decade of professional work, years of teaching, and my own historical research. Good reasons abound to steer students (and clients) away from Futura. The simplest is that the version on most computers is woefully incomplete. The basic version contains only four styles (Medium, *Medium Oblique*, Medium Condensed, and *Medium Condensed Oblique*) instead of a full family, which makes it hard to create typographic contrast and hierarchy—both mainstays of good design. As a text face, Futura can be a difficult typeface to master. With proportionally short x-heights, it can be hard to use at small sizes.

But even armed with these practical reasons, I started to wonder as I began preparing lectures: Was it still good advice? How could I convince my students? And even if it now seemed instinctual to tell young designers not to use Futura for practical reasons, what *does* make Futura work? The question of whether, or when, to use Futura reflects more fundamental questions across design teaching and practice: How do I pick and use the right typeface? When can a popular typeface fail? Where does a typeface's historical or cultural importance fit into its current use?

This question of typeface use, with all of its cultural, historical, and visual baggage, enticed me enough to spend a year in history research at the University of Chicago. During one study session, in the bowels of the Regenstein Library stacks, I went browsing for type specimens. In seeking them out, I stumbled across shelves of books about books. I would have blown past the bibliographic indexes and style guides if it hadn't been for a few trade titles nearby that I recognized from years of working in graphic design: *Communication Arts*, *Print*, and *Graphis*. Soon I found myself in a haven of once pervasive, now long-forgotten printers' magazines from the late nineteenth and early twentieth centuries: *American Printer and Lithographer*, the *Penrose Annual*, and the *Inland Printer*.

Cracking open those pages transported me through time and space. The articles read like design blogs of the present in topic and tone, but within an unfamiliar setting: they were printed on dusty cotton sheets in a stodgy cut of Bodoni instead of the sleek cascading style sheets of a modern browser—no color photos or pop-up adverts in sight. One opinion article in the 1930 issue of the *Inland Printer* caught my eye: "You Didn't Go Wrong on Modernism if You Followed the *Inland Printer*!" With the familiar vigor of a *Brand New* or *Design Observer* post, this writer had his say against modernism, the biggest trend of the day. Reading this article, and others like it, revealed a debate that history and common practice had all but closed.

In studying old printers' magazines I saw the world before Futura and Helvetica, and, truth be told, before Graphic Design itself. I could imagine the past, when printers still dominated the practice of fine typography or when late nineteenth- and early twentieth-century icons like William Morris and Bruce Rogers remained the transcendent models for contemporary layout. Imagining this past helped me appreciate the bracing newness of a typeface like Futura. Contrary to what I had understood as an undergraduate, the pages of the *Inland Printer* and other trade journals revealed a world where dedicated design practitioners were not all on the side of the Bauhaus, Russian constructivists, or Swiss modernism. The importance of recognizing the past, with its dissidents, countermovements, and reactionaries, should be obvious to any serious student of history, but in current day-to-day life it can be hard to imagine. It is entirely possible that the first letters I ever saw were in Futura, in a children's book or on the sides of crayons. Or if not Futura, on some label in Helvetica. The artifacts of modernism's past are today's ubiquity.

How did Futura become so popular, when it could have been just another trend? New trends in fashion always emerge, usually to be swept aside a few years later. Old masters are supplanted, and most typefaces quickly become associated with moments in time or with particular ideas—whether it is movements like art deco, or imagined pasts like the American Old West, or specific business sectors like late 1970s and early 1980s tech companies, or even today's ubiquitous meme font. Even wildly successful and popular typefaces have life cycles of coolness. They start in cutting-edge magazines like GQ and end when they are found on signs telling employees to wash their hands in the restroom.

Amazingly, even after ninety years of commercial use, Futura has an appeal that seems to be evergreen.

This book was born out of my own experiences grappling with Futura's ongoing popularity and trying to answer the question of when it is appropriate to use with my students and in my own work. Framing the past through this single typeface opens up an alternate history of graphic design and culture. Familiar images created by graphic design legends contrast with the prosaic work of jobbing printers and demonstrate the spread of typographic trends. This history of Futura includes many celebrated examples, but it is also buttressed by ephemera that would otherwise be forgotten, such as highway maps, political pins, brochures, government charts, atlases, calendars, and books. Examining the varied high and low examples of Futura illuminates the vibrant, pervasive function of type in society. Type conveys its own meanings, character, and values in society, beyond just being an artifact of time or place, or a means to some other end.

Each chapter addresses a distinct way that Futura functions as a product of modernism, as an inspiration for copies, as a key component in systems, as distilled ideology and political rhetoric, as commercial branding and advertising, as a means for appropriating, subverting, and commenting on society, and also as a model for new work. The constellation of meanings embedded in the typeface Futura answers the simple question of "what typeface should I use?" by revealing deeper questions: Why and how has a typeface been used in the past? And what ideas is it capable of inhabiting today?

So never use Futura, unless . . .

jazzways

a year book
of hot m
One dollar

MY OTHER MODERNISM IS IN FUTURA

WHEN ALFRED H. BARR promoted modern European art to new audiences in the United States, modern typefaces came along for the ride. In 1936, while preparing a new exhibition titled Cubism and Abstract Art for the Museum of Modern Art in New York City, Barr created a chart to accompany the show to help people understand the many modern art movements that had contributed to abstraction. It connects the different strands—like cubism, futurism, Dadaism, constructivism, surrealism, and the Bauhaus—with one another, across countries, genres, and years. The chart itself was typeset in the most modern typefaces Barr had available, including Futura.[1]

For most Americans, Futura and other new German typefaces were their everyday consumption of modernism. Futura burst into appearance in magazines, books, newspapers, and posters. Its resonance, along with some gutsy advertising by Bauer Type Foundry, asserted Futura's place at the typographic

An early Bauer Type Foundry advertisement for Futura in the United States, 1928

PREVIOUS
Modernism was more fun when it employed Futura. Here Paul Rand uses it as a counterpoint to a playful Picasso-inspired collage for the inaugural cover of Jazzways magazine, 1946.

table, as "The Typeface for Our Time." It was imagined, drawn, named, and advertised as mathematical over cultural, revolutionary over historical, and distinctively "The Type of Today and Tomorrow," unlike new cuts of old classics or romantic remixes of past glories (think Times New Roman, released in 1932).[2]

The thing about Futura that designers like myself know, though, is that some of its letterforms are not as revolutionary as some of Paul Renner's original ideas. It's a compromise, expertly crafted to be commercially viable to the widest possible audience, from art deco acolytes to avant-garde New Typography followers, and even the workaday printer looking to breathe new life into old layouts.

Beginning with his initial drawings in 1924, Renner was attempting to create a new typeface to fit the age. Like his Bauhaus contemporaries, he played with basic geometry—circles, squares, triangles, and straight lines—to compose his first Futura. The allure was clear: simple shapes could be produced mechanically and bore little visceral reference to preindustrial, humancentric modes of production (handwriting, calligraphy), which undergirded centuries of conventional typography.[3]

Instead, he went for even older models: capital letters followed the classical proportions and elemental shapes of roman monumental type; lowercase, the proportions of sixteenth- and seventeenth-century French letters by Claude Garamond and Jean Jannon. The familiar proportions gave Futura additional legibility and accessibility, in contrast with contemporary typographic experiments, and even Futura's competitors, like Kabel and Erbar, both of which had slightly different proportions. In this way, Futura's balance of

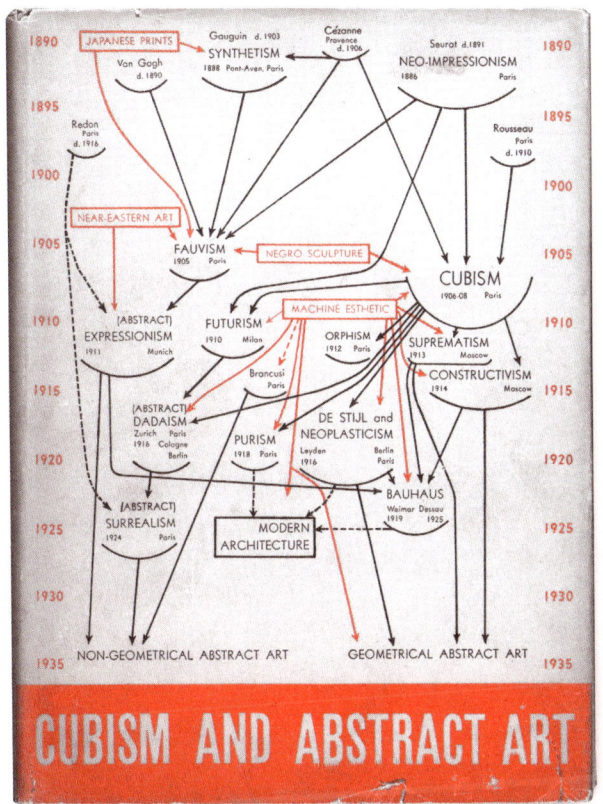

Museum of Modern Art director Alfred H. Barr's Cubism and Abstract Art diagram was one of the first schemas for modern art itself, typset using an Intertype machine in Futura and Vogue (an early Futura competitor in the United States).

tradition and experiment made it revolutionary, pragmatic, and, ultimately, popular.

Some of Renner's early letterforms were extreme, if simple. The lowercase m and n were straight lines and 90-degree angles, the lowercase g was formed from a circle and a triangle, the lowercase a was a circle enclosed by two lines at a right angle, and the lowercase r was a line with a dot next to it. On the lowercase *e*, the horizontal stroke disconnected from the end of the circular stroke, making it look more like a modern Euro symbol than a recognizable letter *e*.*

*Where possible, the early variants of Futura have been placed into the text. Renner's experimental e was not included in the font used (Neufville Digital Futura, 1999).

MY OTHER MODERNISM IS IN FUTURA   27

Early test prints of Futura, 1924–25

In addition to being an endlessly interesting design exercise, Renner's early experimental letters led the way for versions of Futura that undoubtedly sold better, but still hearkened to geometry, modernism, and, above all, form.

In preparation for Futura's commercial release in 1927, Renner and Bauer shelved the extreme letterforms in favor of slightly more conventional and certainly more legible shapes. But printers could still purchase the innovative a, g, m, and n as alternates.[4] Renner and Bauer's iterative approach later became a smug hallmark of Futura's advertising: "The evolution of such a face entailed endless refinements... involved rejection after rejection before the final effects were achieved that justified Futura's immediate acceptance."[5]

At first glance, almost all the letters in the 1927 Futura look like strict compass-and-ruler formations. In the first two weights, Light and Medium, the roman capitals form familiar shapes: a circular O, a sharp triangular M and A, an R made from a half-circle and straight lines, a T that is two straight lines, and a half-circle D. The letters seem precise, with mechanical monolinear strokes and little variation. And yet, at its heart, Futura is not only geometric. The letters E, F, L, and P reveal the classical double-square proportions essential to the entire typeface. The result marries the avant-garde concern with line, shape, and form to millennia-old typographic traditions.[6]

The final letterforms support a facade of strict geometry that masks the sophistication of the letterforms. Many of the changes are subtle deviations from mathematical purity that are essential for obtaining the right visual effect. It's like the extra space on the bottom part of a matte in a picture frame: even if all sides are mathematically equal, if you don't account for visual weight, the frame looks wrong. In well-drawn geometric typefaces, visual sleights of hand abound to ensure the type looks right. The capital O, for example, looks like a circle but is actually ever so slightly wider than it is tall. The sharp tops of the uppercase A, M, and N overshoot the height of the other capital letters to compensate for the thinning lines. And the curved strokes of the lowercase letters thin ever so slightly as they join the straight lines in the letters a, b, d, g, m, n, p, q, and r. The extra weight where a curve joins a straight stroke would appear too thick otherwise, especially at small sizes. These and many other careful deviations from mechanically calculated shapes help make Futura a great typeface.

Bauer Futura Medium, 30-point type at 200 percent. Note how the overshoots visually compensate for the thinning strokes.

The type family grew with additional styles available for sale: a set of decorative geometric shapes called Futura Schmuck (1927), followed quickly by Futura Bold (1928). Empowered by commercial success, the family expanded to include additional weights: Futura Black (1929), followed by Futuras Semibold, Semibold Oblique, Light Oblique, Medium Oblique, Semibold Condensed, and Bold Condensed (1930); Futura Book and Futura Inline (1932); Futura Display (1932); Futura Bold Oblique (1937); Futura Book Oblique (1939); Futura Light Condensed (1950); and Futura Kräftig (1954)—literally, "Futura Strong," effectively a weight somewhere between Semibold and Bold.[7]

The typefaces normally considered to be part of the core Futura family have greater differences between weights than most contemporary type families. For example, the Light and Medium weights have the sharp corners on capitals **A**, **M**, and **N**, which are abandoned for a flat apex in Futura Bold (1928) and most of the other weights. And for good reason: the flat apex helps the bolder weights achieve maximum boldness without sacrificing legibility.

Other styles of Futura are completely different, and many digital versions rarely offer them as part of the family. Futura Black, released in 1929, is a stencil constructed out of abstract shapes that is similar to typefaces associated with art deco and the Roaring Twenties. Some contemporaries derided the entire trend with the racially tinged label *jazz types* and tarred designs using it or similar faces as "loud, black, erratic."[8] Futura Display (1932) is a bold headline typeface based on a rounded rectangular geometry, but unlike the other weights, it has no circular shapes. In the 1950s Renner created another condensed typeface similar to Futura Display that included italics and various weights. It was

OPPOSITE
Futura has greater differences between weights than many current type families. Compare Light to Bold to Black of Bauer Futura as published in *The Typesetters' Book (Das Buch des Setzers)*, 1936.

Futura, mager   4/6-84 Punkt   Light, 1927

Botanischer Garten

Futura, halbfett   4/6-84 Punkt   Medium, 1927

Musik von Händel

Futura, dreiviertelfett   6-84 Punkt   Semibold, 1929

Presse und Kultur

Futura, fett   6-84 Punkt   Bold, 1928

Bücherfreunde

Futura, schmalfett   6-84 Punkt   Bold Condensed, 1930

Zeichnung von Rubens

Futura, schräg mager   6-48 Punkt   Light Oblique, 1930

Dekorative Malerei

Futura, schräg halbfett   6-48 Punkt   Medium Oblique, 1930

Moderne Reklame

Futura Buchschrift   6-14 Punkt   Book, 1932

Katechismus der bildenden Künste

Futura Black   20-84 Punkt   Black, 1929

Seidenindustrie

Futura, licht   20/16-84/72 Punkt   Inline, 1932

SCHWARZWALD

ABCDEFGHIJKLMNO
PQRSTUVWXYZÄÖÜ
abcdefghijklmnopqrſst
uvwxyzäöü ch ck ff fi fl ff ffi ffl ß
1234567890 &.,-:;·!?'(*†«»§
1234567890

ABCDEFGHIJKLMNO
PQRSTUVWXYZÄÖÜ
abcdefghijklmnopqrſst
uvwxyzäöü ch ck ff fi fl ff ffi ffl ß
1234567890 &.,-:;·!?'(*†«»§
1234567890

ABCDEFGHIJKLMNO
PQRSTUVWXYZÄÖÜ
abcdefghijklmnopq
rſstuvwxyzäöü ch ck
ff fi fl ff ffi ffl ß
1234567890
&.,-:;·!?'(*†«»§

released under various names, as Bauer Topic (in the United States and United Kingdom), Vox (Spain), Zénith (France), and Steile Futura (Germany), demonstrating that the name Futura was, above all else, a marketing tool.[9]

Futura was created during an era when typefaces were on the front lines of culture. In 1920s Germany even the alphabet was a matter of national identity and fierce debate. For some traditionalists, the only true German letters were blackletter types like Fraktur—the thick-lined, heavily ligatured types that mimicked medieval scholarly handwriting, in which paper was scarce and words were long. Once popular across Europe, blackletter type was born in Gutenburg's Germany and matured in Luther's Bible. Over the centuries many European nations adopted roman (Latin) typefaces from Italian printers, relegating blackletter to newspaper mastheads and the occasional official document, but Germany had largely resisted the change. In contrast, liberal-minded reformers wanted Germany to integrate with Europe and the Western world by embracing roman typefaces. For reformers, roman types represented a positive attitude toward internationalism, commerce, and science. For traditionalists and nationalists, they posed a cultural threat to the core of German identity. Even the handwriting taught in schools became a contest between Kurrentscript (known as Deutsche Schrift—"German Script") and Latin Script.[10]

Thus, creating a new typography seemed to be an ideal way to change the world for many printers and artists, and their argument was at the forefront of the cultural battles of the day. For Jan Tschichold, typography was the means to create a true socialist

OPPOSITE:
The first three weights of Bauer Futura: Light, Medium, and Bold (1928 specimen)

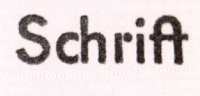

Bauer Futura contains a few characters that reveal its German origins—including *ch* and *ck* ligatures. (8-point type at 300 percent from *Die Kunst der Typographie*, 1940.)

German typefoundries provided a large variety of blackletter typefaces, including various Frakturs.

paradise, imbued with a universal egalitarianism, devoid of class and national distinctions.[11] In 1925 he wrote, "The exclusive materials of New Typography are those given by the task…. Ornament of even the simplest form (shaded rules!) is superfluous, impermissible." Importantly, the typefaces mattered: "The simplest and therefore only persuasive form of European script is the Block—(sans serif)—type…. National typefaces are excluded as generally incomprehensible and as leftovers from history."[12] The

bahnhofsplatz
Abb. 3. Versuch einer neuen Schrift von Herbert Bayer

einfacher Elemente
Abb. 4. „Schablonenschrift" von Josef Albers

NEUE PLASTISCHE SYSTEMSCHRIFT
Abb. 5. „Systemschrift" von Kurt Schwitters

Internationale Buchkunst-Ausstellung

Das Gutenberg-Denkmal in Mainz
Abb. 6. „Futura"- Schrift von Paul Renner

Comparison of geometric typefaces by Herbert Bayer, Josef Albers, and Kurt Schwitters with Futura in *Klimschs Jahrbuch*, 1928

printed form of Tschichold's manifesto makes clear that these national typefaces included Fraktur and German blackletters, as well as Russian Cyrillic types, and any other distinctive national scripts.

Others in the debate pushed for radical equality in the Latin alphabet as well. Herbert Bayer, a student and teacher at the Bauhaus, pushed for a single roman lowercase alphabet—no capitals—to replace the traditional two-case alphabet. Bayer theorized that the two-case system lengthened the time it took for children to learn to read, because they had to learn two symbols for every letter. Bayer's design for a single alphabet has a similar starting point as Renner's Futura, built from simple geometric shapes. Appropriately enough, he called his 1925 experimental type design Universal. Bayer's typeface never enjoyed commercial release, but he wasn't alone in advocating such changes. The British writer T. S. Eliot had attempted to eliminate national pride by putting

love, and the gentleman w

from which it is proved that love always seems a little more alluring when it is allied to elegance and good manners

■ How old was I when this incident, of which I am about to tell you, occurred? Eight or nine, perhaps ten. . . . I was a vigorous, noisy child, happiest when, with my comrades, I was engaged in some strenuous, shouting game. Breathless, we loved to tumble over each other in tremendous scuffles, to run all over the countryside in the warm sunlight, playing at robbers and police . . . everyone wanted to run with the robbers—delightful, dangerous creatures whose peril lent them a kind of glamour which the pursuers, clothed in the dull armour of the law, could never hope to possess. We stole birds' nests, we hurled pebbles from our sling-shots far into the smiling sky. . . . Girls did not interest us. They were an inferior sex and for us without attraction. I could not have been ten years old.

However, at about this time I began to observe certain things, to develop a kind of thoughtfulness. It must have been that without realizing I began to see clearly and to ponder upon what I saw; certainly my first impressions of the little town where I was born and of the society in which I grew up were extraordinarily distinct—for, to this day, they remain in my mind's eye sharp and clear, undimmed by the many years between.

■ There was in our town in France one man whom I remember more clearly than any other for, accidentally, he became connected in my mind with the first revelations of a world, a life entirely new to the child that I was then; romantic, mysterious, and passionately interesting, he is forever identified with a moment in my life which I shall never forget.

This man, in our small community where social distinctions and rank were strongly defined, belonged to one of the old *bourgeois* families of which, for lack of any others, our aristocracy was composed—comfortable land-owners whose ancestors before them had tilled their own soil. But he was startlingly not of them; he was a man apart, a mystery. To begin with he was—at thirty-five—a bachelor, and that in itself was a rare thing in our small, sturdy world where men married young; and not only was he a bachelor but, superbly, he was an idle bachelor. While other men worked at their trades on their farms, he did neither; he was a man of leisure, subsisting on the small income which his father had left him.

This was interesting. In our simple eyes it heightened the distinction that somehow was already his—the elegance that, instinct in his every gesture, reached a glorious climax in the suave glitter of the monocle that he wore. Yes, he wore a monocle. Here was a marvel that, each time I saw him, amazed me anew. With a youthful curiosity, I studied it: his left eye drooped a little, but the right one opened wide behind a circle of glass framed in tortoise-shell and thrust grandly in the arch of his eyebrow. Why, I wondered, didn't it fall out with the jolting of his steps as he walked? That it never did, seemed to me nothing short of miraculous.

He had, furthermore, a taste in dress that was entirely his own, and I still seem to see the richly cut fawn-coloured suit in which he was wont to stroll, fashionable and unique, along the *Grande Rue*. His given name, too, was surprising; for in the heart of our French province he called himself, unaccountably, James. Where, we marveled, had he got this British name when our own fathers were all Jules, Pierre or Jacques?

■ But bachelorhood, idleness, monocle, clothes, British name . . . all of these paled before another and still more enchanting distinction: he wore sideburns! There were, of course, others in the town. The clerk of the court wore in front of his ears two rabbits' paws of a doubtful white, and the cheeks of the tailor in the *Place du Marché* were pallid beneath a startling arrangement of whiskers . . . but what were these compared to the sideburns of this delightful James? Of a dark, gentle brown, they were a mere melancholy shadow on each temple, extending almost to the lobe of the ear and giving his face a rounded, almost a delicate contour. More than that they implied, in our lavishly bearded community, a sense of restraint which was enormously chic. Unique, then, this James with his sideburns, and for me a glamorous and exciting personage whom I looked upon with awe; for in the simple, everyday life of our town, my young eyes saw no other vestige of romance. Life there seemed to me rather tepid and lacking in interest; things happened too regularly. Our people followed a mode of living from which all fantasy seemed necessarily to be excluded. They became engaged, got married and had children who in their turn grew up, became men and women, and continued to lead the identical life that had been their parents' before them—helplessly following the immutable laws, human and divine, which were dutifully observed by all society.

But I had begun to suspect that this most correct outer life and vaguely identified with it, there thing else—something mysterious able which was not mentioned children, but the influence of which was revealed to us with startling name of this mystery, which c scurely in the songs our nurses s and in the refrains of the stre was love.

In our ignorant, boyish language *was I then?*) love meant to pay co that is to say, to stare at them, to p they passed us in the street, to ad boldly, bully them a little, and to all occasions our own masculine s Beyond this we spoke of them scorn. We were, after all, men; and girls. We existed, like the angels, of hierarchy of which we male crea occupied the glorious summit.

■ Was there, perhaps, some occult harmony which love establishe human beings? . . . Ah, how vagu to our eyes of youth! We only love was a mysterious thing, a t from us, carefully hidden from us we hadn't all observed, at one time some farm lad pursuing a flushed ing servant-girl, or a clerk boldly arm about the waist of a girl . . . and sometimes a couple separat when they heard a noisy group out of school, bursting into a shel But that was all. That people o world could ever lend themselves behaviour we did not believe p the simple reason that we had no happen. The gestures of love a

Mehemed Agha's October 1929 *Vanity Fair* redesign brought avant-garde European typography and art to the American mainstream. The redesign was a watershed moment within the spread of a modernist aesthetic. Not all of the ideas were well received. Due to reader outcry, the magazine abandoned the all-lowercase titling in the March 1930 issue.

e monocle

BY CLAUDE ANET

are to be tainted with a certain vulgarity definitely restricted to the lower

he day, I saw an astonishing thing. a late afternoon in the Spring, I he house, my sling-shot in my pocket, gone to a little neighbouring wood in of winging, by a happy shot, some bird. A wild and winding path is wood, a charming, solitary place, fteen minutes' walk from the town, cely anybody came there except on now it was deserted. The rays of g sun danced through the cool, dark a shower of liquid gold; turtle ed in the distance. Warm, and a little had stopped to wait until a blackbird ghest bough of a tree should change on for one more favourable to my aim, when I saw two people entering wood.

e I recognized the magnificent James, smiling, romantic, he advanced rough a charming little pattern of shadow. And at his side there walked Who was she? At that distance, I see, and I was consumed with curiosity hesitatingly, I flung myself behind a r by and, motionless as a crouching I waited.

people drew nearer, and I perceived the lady with the magnificent James cousin by marriage. She was a young married not longer than five or six no had come from a distant province therefore been received by our community with that slight coolness which the bourgeois know so well how to affect. diligently, *(Continued on page 100)*

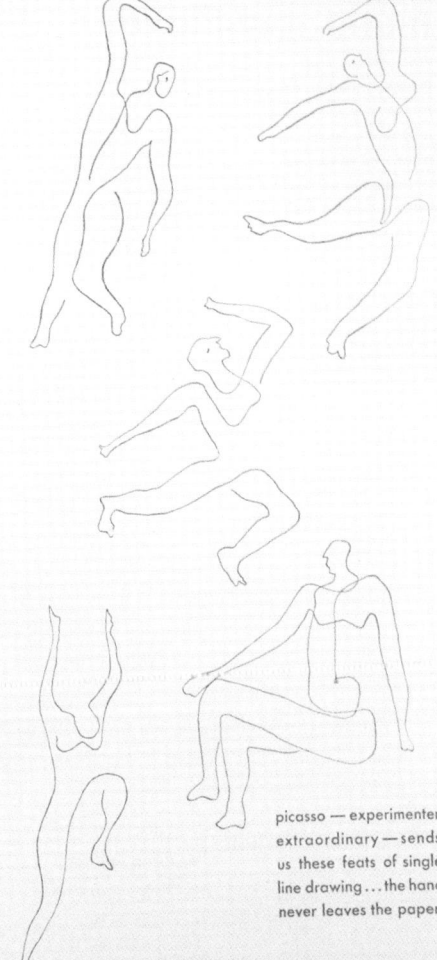

picasso — experimenter extraordinary — sends us these feats of single line drawing ... the hand never leaves the paper!

some one-line drawings by pablo picasso

Agha's redesign of *Vanity Fair* featured Futura and innovative amounts of white space.

nationalities in lowercase, e.g., *the english*, not *the English*—which sounds egalitarian, except when lowercase universalism is shorthand for denigration, as when James Joyce ominously set *jew* instead of *Jew*.[13]

For many, using Futura in print came packaged with these underlying cultural battles about capitalization, nationalism, and modernity. Printers and writers across the United States noted the changes with varying degrees of acceptance. A flashpoint arose in 1929 with the redesign of *Vanity Fair*.

Vanity Fair had redesigned the entire magazine largely in sync with modernist styles. All the headlines for feature stories were set in lowercase, and all the typography throughout the magazine used Futura. The redesign represented one of the first direct incursions of European design into American publications.

The recently hired art director in charge of the redesign, Mehemed Agha, had previously been the director of *Vogue Berlin*.[14] The structure of the contents page, as well as organizational headings, suggests his interest in utilizing elements, such as the typeface Futura and bold rules (lines), that were common in modern European typographic designs.

Agha's expressive typography met with opposition, however, and within five issues the more avant-garde features of the layout were toned down. For example, after the first issue, Agha's layout reverted from all-lowercase titles to once again include upper- and lowercase, and reverted to serifed type rather than sans serif in some aspects of the layout.[15] Responding to readers, the magazine posted a notice that read, in part, "A title set entirely in small letters is unquestionably more attractive than one beginning with a capital or with every word beginning with a capital, but, at the present time, it is also unquestionably harder to read because the eye of the reader is not yet educated to it." Accepting the current state of readership, the text continued: "The issue is thus one between attractiveness and legibility, or between form and content, and *Vanity Fair*, not wishing to undertake any campaign of education, cast its vote by returning to the use of capital letters in titles, to legibility, and to the cause of content above form."[16]

A *New York Times* editorial, "Proletarian Punctuators," satirized the controversy, backlash, and return of capitalization in *Vanity Fair*. The *Times* joked that the "anti-capitalist" lowercase revolution had been compromised with a "New Punctuation Policy," which, like Lenin's New Economic Policy, had reinfused elements of capitalism into a Communist economy. The unchanged left-justified layout is satirized too: "They do not put the name of an article in the centre of the page or in the centre of the column, but put it flush with the left-hand edge of the type column. This revolutionary struggle has maintained itself much more successfully than the case war, by which we mean the war of the lower cases against the upper cases."[17]

Another example of critcism of modernism comes from a 1930 issue of the *Inland Printer*, written by the editor J. L. Frazier.[18] He celebrated the return to traditional orthography as a sane return to legibility, albeit with snide remarks about the magazine's pride in "the chic, the utter modernity of its readers" and its arrogance as the "arbiter elegantiarum."[19] Later Frazier's editorial stand against the excesses of modern experimental design was trumpeted in another *Inland Printer* editorial, "You Didn't Go Wrong on Modernism if You Followed the *Inland Printer*!"[20] It began, "The more intelligent of those persons who two years ago ardently championed the use of the eccentric, malformed, ugly, and illegible type reflecting cubist art, as adding to typography what self-styled modernists called a fresh note, now admit they are passé." The editorial continues to describe the resurgence of traditional norms of printing and, most unsurprisingly, the essential principle of legibility. As such, traditional layout principles are superior to "eccentricities of layout," with "lines and whole displays aslant" and other "bizarre and incomprehensible" characteristics.[21]

Neither Frazier nor the *Inland Printer* were enemies to all new typefaces associated with modernism. Despite its gloating editorials about its abilities

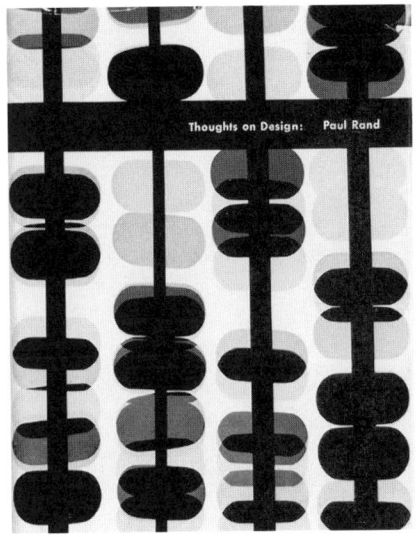 

Paul Rand used Futura in many of his designs, including his 1947 *Thoughts on Design* and his 1957 children's book *Sparkle and Spin*, written with his wife Ann Rand.

to predict trends, even it made a distinction between "cubistic" typefaces and the "smart new 'gothics,'" which are "infinitely more attractive and legible." For Frazier and his editors, one of the benefits of modernism and sans serif typography as opposed to "pseudo-modernists" was "simplicity of layout and absence of ornament."[22] In championing the lack of ornament, the *Inland Printer* defended one of the basic principles that informed both the New Typography of Tschichold and, later, the Swiss style while arguing against the more experimental excesses. Given the gradual adoption of Futura into the headlines of the *Inland Printer* throughout the 1930s, it seems clear that one of the "smart new 'gothics'" must have been Futura. In this light, Frazier's opposition to the *Vanity Fair* redesign seems to have stemmed from his specific opposition to all-lowercase titles and the expansive letterspacing for headlines—both of which violated

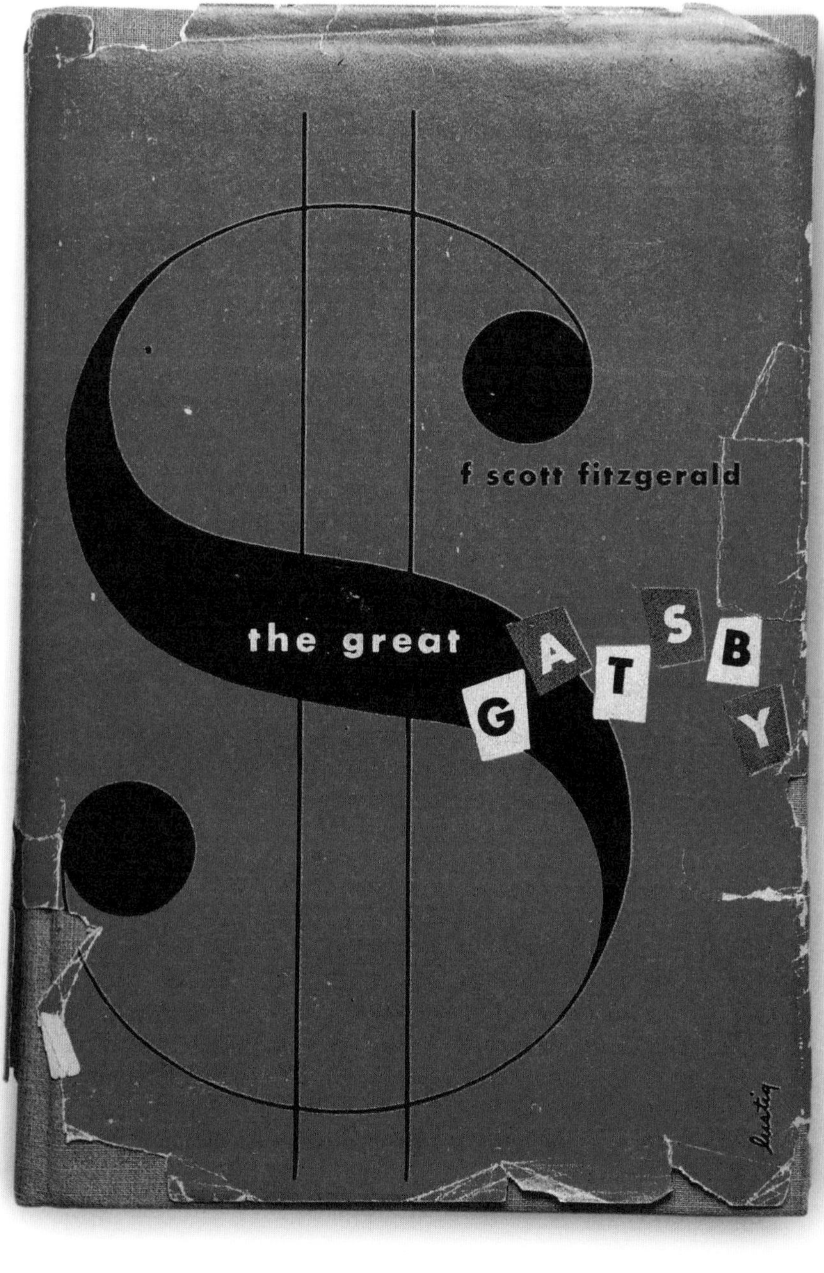

the great **GATSBY**

f scott fitzgerald

OPPOSITE Modernism was more fun when it employed Futura, used here by Alvin Lustig for his cover design for the 1945 reprinting of The Great Gatsby for New Classics, New Directions. The original printed in yellow and black.

ABOVE Herbert Bayer used Futura extensively in his work before and after emigrating from Germany prior to World War II in 1938. His use of the typeface for the Container Corporation of America was part of a unified system to which dozens of illustrators contributed.

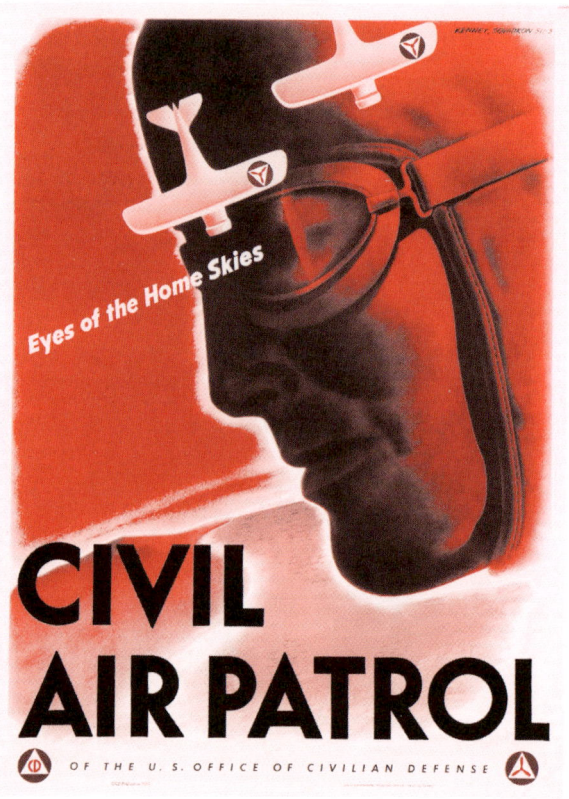

Futura fought on both sides of World War II. American printers, designers, and advertisers largely embraced Futura and new ideas about modernism.

Frazier's sense of legibility—rather than opposition to the typeface Futura.

In America advertisers increasingly specified Futura for printing. All three of the magazines used in the Typographic Scoreboard tabulations by the *Inland Printer*—*Vogue*, the *Saturday Evening Post*, and the *Nation's Business*—showed increases in the use of Futura. *Vogue* in particular demonstrated the greatest change. In 1930 Futura appeared in 18 percent of advertisements in *Vogue* (20 out of 111), compared to

44 NEVER USE FUTURA

8 percent in the *Saturday Evening Post* (21 out of 264).²³ By 1933 *Vogue* advertisements using Futura increased to 23 percent (27 out of 117).²⁴ By 1945 the overall picture of the typographic use demonstrated a complete acceptance of Futura. The *Inland Printer* noted that Futura was featured in one-quarter of all the advertisements (51 out of 210) in three consecutive issues of *Vogue*.²⁵ Bauer ads hyped Futura's advertising success as well, with 1930 ads noting 11 of the 26 full-page ads in the *New Yorker* magazine and 30 of 53 ads in *Harper's Bazaar* featured Futura.²⁶

Many of the most famous designs by American modernist acolytes featured Futura, although often in a supporting role while their illustrative designs and photographs took center stage. Futura was an anchor of many of the works of Paul Rand, Bradbury Thompson, and Alvin Lustig, as well as, with the rise of Nazism in Germany, an expanding number of European émigrés, including Bayer (1938), Ladislav Sutnar (1939), and László Moholy-Nagy (1937)—all of whom brought their own interpretations of modernism to a wide American audience.²⁷

Printers, advertisers, and designers popularized Futura in part because it represented modernity and progress. But for others, Futura simply became a unique headline typeface that could be used in largely traditional layouts with slight modifications. In this way, Futura was completely integrated into a vernacular typography across the country and accepted as an American typeface—even during World War II, in spite of its German roots.²⁸

2

SPARTAN GEOMETRY

IN REALITY, you never have used the real Futura. Even if you still have a drawer of Bauer's lead type, you only have an ancestor of what Futura has become. And unless your name is Erik Spiekermann, even your lead type is likely not authentic. Instead, you've used either a copy—one of Futura's many contemporary competitors created shortly after its release in 1927—or a copy of a copy, one of the dozens of digital Futuras now on the market. Many more knockoffs are just simple reproductions adapted to new formats; many of these even inhabit the name Futura, despite their genealogical or stylistic differences from the Renner/Bauer original. Only experts and wonks can, or want to, tell the difference between the original, the blatant rip-offs, and all the contemporary digital copies. To most viewers, the copies—and even some of the modern hybrids—are Futura.

Futura was never in a class totally of its own. The fact that it persisted and became the modern model of the geometric sans serif is remarkable in itself. Bauer

PREVIOUS
The only Futura that can claim complete authenticity is metal type from Germany's Bauer Type Foundry. Every other Futura, however faithful to the original, is a newer creation.

Look at the foot of the type to identify Bauer Futura in the United States or United Kingdom. Futura (top) exported to those markets had to be milled down (to 0.918 inches high [23.31 mm] from the continental European standard of 0.928 inches [23.56 mm]), unlike American-made type such as Spartan (bottom).

Type Foundry's Futura was only one of many geometric sans serifs to be designed in Germany during the 1920s and '30s. Practically every German company had its own: Ludwig & Mayer's Erbar-Grotesk (1926), Klingspor's Kabel (1927), Berthold's Berthold-Grotesk (1928), Stempel's Elegant-Grotesk (1929) and Neuzeit Grotesk (1932), Schriftguss's Super Grotesk (1930), and Wagner & Schmidt's Kristall Grotesk (1930).[1] All of these typefaces have slightly different proportions, interesting backstories, and unique features to commend them. So how did Futura beat out all its competitors, imitators, and copies to become known as the quintessential geometric sans? In part, good timing.

The aftermath of World War I was a tumultuous time for European economies. In Germany, between 1918 and 1924, the value of the Reichsmark plummeted, with devastating effects for business and industry. In 1924 the US State Department helped arrange an influx of eight hundred million marks into the German economy in an attempt to stabilize postwar European finance, known informally as the Dawes Plan.[2] The loans put a temporary end to Germany's devastating hyperinflation, and helped prime the pump for German war reparation payments to France, Great Britain, and, by extension, the United States.[3] In 1925 a consortium of European typefoundries, including Ludwig & Mayer and Klingspor, capitalized on this infusion of investment and joined the Continental Type Founders Association. They opened an office in New York, giving them the advantage of marketing type directly in the United States. Rather than join the association, Bauer opened its own independent New York office in 1927. Almost immediately, Bauer began marketing and selling a

Kathedrale

Erbar (Ludwig & Mayer), 1926

alten Museum

Kabel Light (Klingspor), 1927

Madrid

Berthold-Grotesk (Berthold), 1928

Elektromechanik

Elegant-Grotesk (Stempel), 1929

new typeface it hoped would be a harbinger of success to come: Futura.

Only Ludwig & Mayer's Erbar, Klingspor's Kabel, and Bauer's Futura were released in the United States during what would become a short window of economic prosperity in the aftermath of World War I. Little did these companies know that there would only be a few short years of stability before the market crash of 1929, and that in 1930 American tariffs would impose barriers to entry for German types not already in the United States. Had Futura been sold a few years before or after, it may never have found a place in the US market. The European geometric sans serifs that were released after Futura barely had a chance.

Yet Futura's success was not just due to good timing. The evidence that Futura was the most popular of its cohort is that it was the most widely imitated.

SPARTAN GEOMETRY 49

SPARTAN

➡ MEDIUM AND MEDIUM ITALIC

Here is a sans serif that brings new utility to a design already established as a composing room standard. Through arrangement with the Mergenthaler Linotype Company, ATF Spartan Medium and Medium Italic match the machine versions in the smaller sizes, and extend their design characteristics in the larger sizes. The harmony between machine-set body matter and hand-set display thus obtainable is but one of the many features of the ATF Spartans. Designers and layout men will appreciate their careful fitting and the convenience of the auxiliaries cut to go with them. Compositors will look on these auxiliaries as time-savers and find similar economy in the fact that these faces are cast on American line. Printers will be quick to recognize all these advantages but will set even greater store by the accurate casting and the wearability that make ATF type "the best type made."

AMERICAN TYPE FOUNDERS
ELIZABETH, NEW JERSEY

Branches and Selling Agents in Twenty-three Principal Cities

In 1939 Linotype released Spartan, the company's answer to Futura, on its linecasting machines, and worked with American Type Founders to release Spartan in foundry type so that it could compete on all printing systems.

FUTURA

Futura (Bauer, Paul Renner in foundry type, licensed to Intertype for compositing), 1927

MAKE TROUBLE

Vogue (Intertype), 1930

CONCERT

Spartan (Linotype for compositing and American Type Founders for foundry type), 1939

SELECT WRITER

Tempo (Ludlow, R. Hunter Middleton), 1930

PRINTING

Twentieth Century (Lanston Monotype, Saul Hess), 1937

AXYZazbc5

Airport Gothic (Baltimore Type), 1927–28

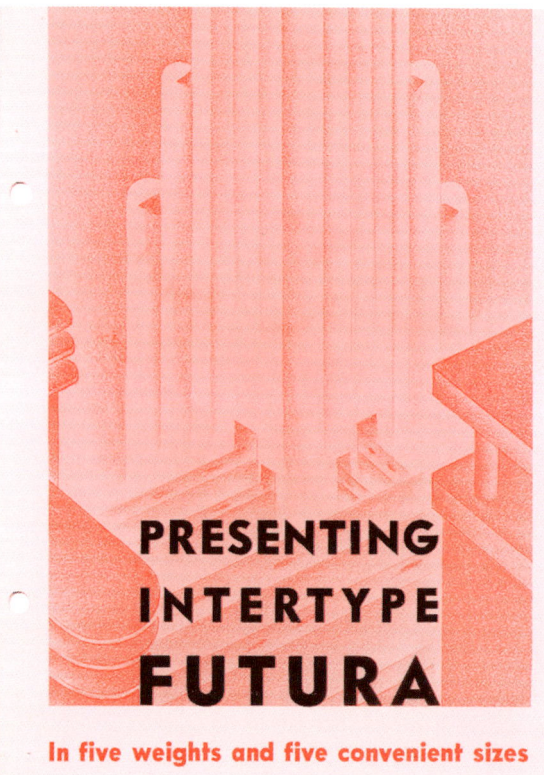

ABOVE
Intertype licensed the name Futura for its typecasting machines in 1934. Even though it is nominally Futura, this design is actually Intertype's Vogue. Later versions had greater fidelity to Bauer Futura.

ABOVE RIGHT
Linotype's Metro, as first released in 1929

Within a year of its release, Futura had already been ripped off. To meet American market demand, the Baltimore Type Foundry created an indistinguishable copy called Airport Gothic. (Sources vary on the details: it was either copied from smuggled drawings of the original or, more likely, electrotyped from the Bauer metal castings). The successful use of Futura in the October 1929 *Vanity Fair* redesign prompted its art director, Mehemed Agha, to commission a custom version of Futura called Vogue for a similar redesign of *Vogue* magazine. Designed by Intertype in 1930, the custom typeface was created in part to achieve compatibility with the company's compositing machines (and no doubt to avoid licensing fees).

Linotype, not wanting to miss the new demand, commissioned the famed type designer W. A. Dwiggins to design a new sans serif typeface. Dwiggins created a truly original design called Metro, based loosely on geometric principles but with humanistic strokes, released in 1929. Yet within a year, commercial pressure forced Dwiggins to make changes to get Metro to look more like Futura: a single-story **a** and sharp pointed tips to the angular strokes of **M** and **N**. Released in 1930, Metro No. 2 is likely the only version of Metro that you've ever seen, as it quickly eclipsed the original in popularity.

In 1930 the Chicago-based designer Robert Hunter Middleton created his own Futura-like design called Tempo for Ludlow. Breaking from the geometric rigidity of Futura, many of Tempo's italic capitals feature a slight curve. The wavelike shapes give Tempo a light, warm, and breezy air absent from the mechanical precision of Futura. This is especially true with the "cursive capitals" alternate letters in display sizes, which give the type a distinct and friendly look. And yet, bending to market pressures, Ludlow released Tempo with enough alternate characters to instantly dress it up to look like Kabel or Futura.

By 1937 Futura's popularity was extensive enough that Linotype's competitor, Lanston Monotype, marketed its own slavish copy of Futura called Twentieth Century for its machines. The same year, Intertype, a close rival of Linotype machines, managed to secure a license from Bauer to make Futura on its own system of linecasting type machines.

Linotype Metro
Linotype Metro No. 2

60 and 72 Point
Ludlow 28-LI Tempo Light Italic

IDEAL TYPE F(
Better Display
delicate charac

The standard characters of Ludlow Tempo are similar to Futura. But in display sizes, Tempo included the unique "cursive capitals."

SPARTAN GEOMETRY 53

MONOTYPE RECORDER

SERIES No. 262
ROMAN

A	a	b	d	g	J	M	N	p
581	166	131	307	70	83	165	210	275

Q	q	R	s	t	u	W	w	W
91	168	199	439	288	346	109	110	153

TOP Gill Sans (1928), designed by Eric Gill for Monotype, was British Monotype's (mostly) successful answer to the demand for new sans serifs. Even today, Gill Sans continues to dominate the English cultural landscape. **ABOVE** Yet, to meet market demand, alternate letters sold by British Monotype styled Gill Sans like Futura (and Kabel).

Vogue 10 point

ABCDEFGHIJKLMNOPQRSTUVWXYZ
abcdefghijklmnopqrstuvwxyz   1234567890
[]%†§‡¶*()$,.-;':'!?&⅛¼⅜½⅝¾⅞

Special No. 2   Special No. 6   Special No. 8
GQ ɢǫ afgtu"1   Gag;   kmnru

Special No. 3
CGJMQUWY cɢjmǫwy abcefgijrt,.;"12

Special No. 4 Small Caps
ABCDEFGHIJKLMNOPQRSTUVWXYZ

ABOVE Alternate characters allow Vogue to look like Futura and Kabel. Special No. 2 dresses the typeface as Futura, and Special No. 3 as Kabel.

OPPOSITE Who owns the shape of the alphabet? Typically, only the name of a typeface is granted copyright. Baltimore Type Company's Airport Gothic (1928) is among the first pirated copies of Futura.

TYPE BETTER TYPE **BALTOTYPE**

Airport Gothic   No. 102

─────── CHARACTERS IN COMPLETE FONT ───────

ABCDEFGHIJKLMNOPQRSTUV
WXYZ&abcdefghijklmnopqrstu
vwxyz.,-':;?!fiffflffl($1234567890

*6 Pt.—40A CAPS 80a Lower Case
ABCDEFGHIJKLMNOPQRSTUVWXYZABCDEabcdefghijklmnopqrstuvwxyzabcdef$12345

*8 Pt.—30A CAPS 60a Lower Case
ABCDEFGHIJKLMNOPQRSTUVWXYZABCabcdefghijklmnopqrstuvwxyz $13

*9 Pt.—26A CAPS 53a Lower Case
ABCDEFGHIJKLMNOPQRabcdefghijklmnopqrstuvwxyz $1234567

*10 Pt.—26A CAPS 53a Lower Case
ABCDEFGHIJKLMNOPQRSTUabcdefghijklmnopqrstuv $123

*11 Pt.—24A CAPS 47a Lower Case
ABCDEFGHIJKLMNabcdefghijklmnopqrstuvwy $12345

*12 Pt.—24A CAPS 47a Lower Case
AVWXYZABCDEFGHIJKLavwxyzabcdefghijkl $23

14 Pt.—22A CAPS 42a Lower Case
ABCDEFGHIJKLMNOabcdefghijklmnop $12

18-1 Pt.—12A CAPS 26a Lower Case
AMNOPQRSTUValmnopqrstuv $78

18-2 Pt.—12A CAPS 26a Lower Case
AWXYZABCDEFawxzabcdef $90

24 Pt.—8A CAPS 17a Lower Case
AGHIJKLMNafghijklmn $12

30 Pt.—6A CAPS 10a Lower Case
AOPQRSTaopqrstu 3

36 Pt.—5A CAPS 7a Lower Case
AUVWavwxy 4

42 Pt.—4A CAPS 6a Lower Case
ABCDabcei 28

48 Pt.—4A CAPS 6a Lower Case
AXYZazbc 5

Airport Gothic Italic   No. 202

─────── CHARACTERS IN COMPLETE FONT ───────

ABCDEFGHIJKLMNOPQRSTUVW
XYZ&abcdefghijklmnopqrstuv
wxyz.,-':;?!fiffflffl)$1234567890

*6 Pt.—40A CAPS 80a Lower Case
ABCDEFGHIJKLMNOPQRSTUVWXYZABCDEabcdefghijklmnopqrstuvwxyzabcdefgh$12345

*8 Pt.—30A CAPS 60a Lower Case
AFGHIJKLMNOPQRSTUVWXYZABCahijklmnopqrstuvwxyzabcdefgh$167890

*9 Pt.—26A CAPS 53a Lower Case
ABCDEFGHIJKLMNOPQRSTUVWXYZabcdefghijklmnopqrstu $1234

*10 Pt.—26A CAPS 53a Lower Case
ABCDEFGHIJKLMNOPQRSTUWabcdefghijklmnopqrstuv $123

*11 Pt.—24A CAPS 47a Lower Case
ABCDEGHILMNOPRSTWYabcdefghiklmnoprstuw $123

*12 Pt.—24A CAPS 47a Lower Case
AVWXYZABCDEFGHIJKLawxyzabcdefghijklm $45

14 Pt.—22A CAPS 42a Lower Case
ABCDEFGHIJKLMNabcdefghijklmnoqp $123

18-1 Pt.—12A CAPS 26a Lower Case
AMNOPQRSTUVanopqrsuvwxyz $78

18-2 Pt.—12A CAPS 26a Lower Case
AWXYZABCDEFazabcdefghij $90

24 Pt.—8A CAPS 17a Lower Case
AGHIJKLMNaklmnopqr $12

30 Pt.—6A CAPS 10a Lower Case
AOPQRSTastuvwx 3

36 Pt.—5A CAPS 7a Lower Case
AUVWayzabc 4

48 Pt.—4A CAPS 6a Lower Case
AXYZadeg 5

OPPOSITE
A 1939 boycott urged US printers to choose American-made typefaces, even if the designs themselves largely followed German fashions.

By 1939 Linotype realized that their redesigned Metro was not enough to meet the demand for a Futura-like typeface. In response to the company's tactical defeat, it created an expansive type family called Spartan that was largely indistinguishable from Futura. To help it fully compete in the market, Linotype partnered with American Type Founders to make matching foundry type. In one small difference, however, Linotype's Spartan included the alternate lowercase double-story *a* on request.

Within a decade of Futura's release, every major American type company now had a Futura-like typeface in its catalog. Even with many excellent competing geometric sans serifs, Europe wasn't immune to the spread of Futura copies. In 1930 the preeminent French foundry, Deberny & Peignot, licensed a copy of Futura and released it under the name Europe.

In the United Kingdom, British Monotype seemed to blunt the march of Futura and the other German sans serifs with the success of Gill Sans (1928), an updated version of Edward Johnston's Underground typeface (1918) by his protégé Eric Gill. Yet even British taste bowed to German influence. Like Linotype had with Metro and Ludlow with Tempo, British Monotype released alternate characters to help Gill Sans match the Futura look.

Back in America, even with all the Futura copies, and despite new tariffs on American goods, the original—Bauer's Futura—remained a bestseller. It success is partly evidenced by the fact that it merited a boycott: in 1939 major American printers, advertisers, and publishers united to ban typefaces from Nazi Germany. Rather than send American dollars to fund Nazi aggression, they called for spending

Nazi-Made Types

ADASTRA
ALLEGRO
AMBASSADOR
ARISTON
ATRAX
BALLE INITIALS
BAUER TEXT
BAYER
BERNHARD BOOK
" BRUSHSCRIPT
" CURSIVE
" ROMAN and ITAL.
BETON series
BODONI (Bauer)
CANDIDA
CARTOON
CITY COMPACT
CLAUDIUS
CORVINUS
DAPHNIS
DIANE
EDITOR
ELAN DEMI-BOLD
ELIZABETH
EVE
FUTURA series
GILLIES GOTHIC
GIRDER series
GLADIOLA
HOLLA
KABEL series
LEGEND
LILITH
LUCIAN
LUXOR BOLD COND.
MARATHON
MAXIMILIAN
MERIDIAN
METROPOLIS
MONDIAL
NARCISSUS
NEULAND
OFFENBACH
ORPHEUS
PHYLLIS
SIGNAL
SKETCH
SLENDER
TIEMANN
TRAFTON
VIKING
WEISS (Bauer)
ZEPPELIN

Boycott Nazi Type!

EVERY TIME you order a German-made type face, American dollars go abroad to help Nazi aggression. All branches of the graphic arts are joining in a concerted movement to ban the use of type faces made in Nazi Germany. Boycotting Nazi type faces does not mean sacrificing artistic merit. American-made types are available to replace the most commonly-used Nazi faces.

By specifying American type faces you will help American industry and further the development of American type design. Reference to your type specimen books will reveal many American type faces you may have overlooked which can be used in place of Nazi-made types.

Specify type **"NOT MADE IN GERMANY."**

Made in Germany	Made in U.S.A.
FUTURA series	20th CENTURY series (Mono.)
	SPARTAN series (Lino.)
	VOGUE series (Intertype)
	TEMPO series (Ludlow)
FUTURA Display	Tourist Gothic · Othello
KABEL series	SANS SERIF series (Mono.)
BETON series	STYMIE series (A.T.F.)
	STYMIE series (Mono.)
BETON OPEN	CAIRO OPEN
GIRDER series	KARNAK series (Ludlow)
	MEMPHIS series (Lino.)
	CAIRO series (Intertype)
Bernhard Cursive	Liberty
Bernhard Roman and Italic	Bernhard Modern and Italic
LUCIAN · **Lucian Bold**	GRAPHIC Light · **GRAPHIC Bold**
BODONI TYPES (Bauer)	BODONI TYPES (American)
CARTOON	**COMIQUE · FLASH · BALLOON**
Eve Light · *Eve Italic*	Rivoli · *Rivoli Italic*
Eve Heavy	Paramount
NEULAND	**NORWAY · NEWTOWN**
OFFENBACH	LYDIAN
Gillies Gothic Bold	**Kaufmann Bold**
Signal	Britannic · *Swing Bold*
AMBASSADOR II	LYDIAN *Italic*
ATRAX	HOMEWOOD
CORVINUS	EDEN
Gladiola	*Romany*
Holla	*Keynote*
Mondial Bold Condensed	**Ultra Bodoni Extra Condensed**
Narcissus	Narciss · Cameo · Gravure
Trafton	Coronet

Encourage American Design!

Semplicità, designed by Alessandro Butti for the Italian typefoundry Nebiolo, 1930

Grotesca Radio, designed by Spanish typefoundy Fundación Tipográfica de Richard Gans, c. 1930

Granby, designed by British typefoundry Stephenson Blake, 1930

UNIVERSUM

ELEGANTE TIPO DE ACTUALIDAD Y DEL PORVENIR

AAA BB CC DD EEEE FF G G HH III JJ KK LLL MM NN N OOO PP Q RRR SSS TTT UU VV WW X Y Y Z & ,,, ; : ...

money on American typefaces. To "avoid sacrificing artistic merit," they provided a guide of American substitutes—composed of Futura-inspired copies and knockoffs—and proved Futura was more than just another competing typeface.[4]

America's entry into World War II in 1941 ended what little trade remained between the United States and Germany. By all rights, the end of trade and anti-German war propaganda should have killed the Futura brand forever in favor of an American knock-off or competitor. Yet by 1941 the aesthetic idea of Futura was too big to die: even American military propaganda posters and US military war maps utilized Futura or, more likely, its American copies.

Even though fresh metal cases of Bauer Futura were unavailable during the war, Futura as an idea persisted in its competitors and copies. By the 1950s, when anti-German sentiments had quieted and German-American trade had resumed, Bauer's Futura enjoyed an easy reentry into the American market, where demand for the product, name, and aesthetic had never died. By the mid-1950s Futura was still the established brand leader in the United States, despite a decade of near-exclusive availability of American versions.

For example, when advertisers and designers called their local typesetting offices, sometimes they didn't even have a clear choice of typeface. Since each variation worked in slightly different machines and systems, it was better business to sell only the general category rather than specific typefaces. In Baltimore, typesetting companies listed their geometric typefaces as "Futuria" instead of Tempo, Airport Gothic, Spartan, or Twentieth Century. Others occasionally even listed Kabel and Gill Sans under the Futura title. Sure, some designers could still specify Futura instead of Futuria, but that was like trying to use Helvetica Neue instead of Arial on Google Docs today—the system is just not built for it.

Given Futura's status as the brand leader for the category of geometric sans serifs, new copies of Futura were made for each new typesetting system. Futura was one of the first typefaces adapted for new phototypesetting machines as well as later digital fonts for desktop publishing. While some of the non-Futura copies received their own photo or digital updates, others were simply forgotten. Eventually some competitors bent to commercial pressure and

Typesetting companies often created their own specimens and used the names they found most appropriate. Above, Ludlow's Tempo is branded as Futura.

FUTURA MEDIUM No. 815 CLASS O
(Cut in sizes from 4 line to 36 line)

FOUR LINE

ABCDEFGHIJKLT$&,.?!

FOUR LINE

Rabcdefghijklmnopqrst

HAMILTON MANUFACTURING COMPANY • Two Rivers, Wisconsin

SIX LINE *See explanation of point width table on Page 4.*

EGABMRYSO

EIGHT LINE

RILNODUF

TEN LINE

QUENIB

PAGE 10

TABLE OF APPROXIMATE CHARACTER POINT-WIDTHS

FUTURA MEDIUM No. 815		A	B	C	D	E	F	G	H	I	J	K	L	M	N	O	P	Q	R	S	T	U	V	W	X	Y	Z	&	.	,	!	?	1	2	3	4	5	6	7	8	9	0	$
FOUR LINE	U.C.	44.0	29.0	27.5	26.5	26.5	24.0	46.5	35.0	8.0	20.5	34.5	22.0	52.5	41.5	48.0	27.5	49.0	31.0	28.5	34.5	41.0	65.5	58.5	37.0	34.5	42.5		8.5	12.5	9.0	24.0	14.5	32.0	32.0	34.0	32.5	34.0	30.5	32.5	33.5	28.5
	L.C.	31.0	31.5	26.0	31.5	29.0	19.0	31.5	26.5	8.0	9.5	26.5	6.5	46.0	26.5	32.0	31.5	31.5	20.0	22.0	15.5	26.0	30.0	47.5	33.0	32.5	31.5																
FIVE LINE	U.C.	55.0	36.0	47.0	45.5	33.0	30.0	58.5	44.0	10.5	25.5	43.0	27.5	66.0	52.0	61.0	34.0	61.0	39.0	36.0	43.0	51.5	82.0	45.5	46.0	43.0	53.0		10.5	15.5	11.0	30.0	18.0	40.0	40.0	43.5	41.0	41.0	38.0	40.0	42.0	35.5
	L.C.	36.5	39.5	32.5	39.5	36.5	23.5	39.5	33.0	10.0	11.5	33.0	7.0	57.0	33.5	40.0	39.0	39.0	25.0	27.5	19.5	32.0	37.5	59.5	41.0	40.5	39.5																
SIX LINE	U.C.	66.0	43.5	56.5	54.5	40.0	36.0	70.0	52.5	12.5	30.5	51.5	33.0	75.0	63.0	73.0	41.0	73.0	47.0	47.0	47.0	43.0	51.5	62.0	98.5	54.5	55.5	51.5	63.5	12.5	18.5	13.5	36.0	21.5	48.0	48.0	52.0	49.5	49.0	51.0	45.5	48.0	50.5	42.5
	L.C.	46.5	47.0	39.0	47.0	43.5	28.5	47.0	40.0	12.0	14.0	39.5	12.0	68.5	40.0	48.0	47.0	47.0	30.5	33.0	23.5	38.5	45.0	71.0	49.0	48.5	47.0																
EIGHT LINE	U.C.	88.0	58.0	75.0	72.5	53.0	48.0	93.5	70.0	16.5	40.5	68.5	43.5	105	83.0	97.5	54.5	97.5	62.5	62.5	57.5	69.0	82.5	131	72.5	74.0	69.0	84.5	17.0	25.0	18.0	48.5	28.5	64.0	64.0	68.5	66.0	65.5	68.0	61.0	63.5	67.5	56.5
	L.C.	61.5	63.0	52.0	63.0	58.0	37.5	63.0	53.0	16.5	18.5	52.5	17.5	91.5	53.5	64.0	62.5	62.5	40.0	44.0	31.5	51.5	60.0	95.0	65.5	64.5	63.0																
TEN LINE	U.C.	110	72.5	94.0	90.5	66.5	60.0	116	87.5	20.5	50.5	85.5	54.5	132	103	121	66.5	122	78.0	78.0	71.5	86.0	103	164	90.5	92.5	86.0	106	21.0	31.5	22.5	60.5	35.5	80.0	80.0	95.5	82.5	81.5	85.0	75.0	79.5	84.5	70.5
	L.C.	77.0	78.5	65.0	78.5	72.5	47.0	78.5	66.0	20.5	23.5	66.5	21.5	114	66.5	80.0	78.0	78.0	50.0	55.0	39.0	64.5	75.0	118	82.0	81.0	78.5																

OPPOSITE Hamilton Manufacturing Company manufactured their wood type version of Futura (1951) for printers to use on posters, placards, and flyers.

ABOVE Other companies created their own wood type Futura knockoffs, including Acme's Moderna (1937) and American Wood Type's Mode (1936).

No digital Futuras are exactly alike. In red is Neufville Digital's Futura; the other outlines are a dozen contemporary Futuras, each in the same point size.

licensed the name Futura from Bauer, completing the hegemony of idea over the true product. Linotype's phototypesetting typeface was not Spartan; it was just Futura.

In an age of open software and open type, the new legends are made from people and designs that are virally copied, shared, and used as templates. In this vein, it is appropriate that today Futura's popularity continues through its dozens of digital copies. Every major type company of the last twenty years has its own licensed version: Bitstream Futura,

Adobe Futura, Paratype Futura, Elser & Flake Futura, Neufville Digital Futura, Berthold Futura, and even Monotype Futura and Linotype Futura. The idea of a geometric sans serif and its name are now so powerfully linked that people want Futura—not a substitute. Even though we now buy Futura from any number of companies, all of them send royalties back to the Renner family for the Futura name, in licensed trademarks of Bauer types.[5]

Futura as the enduring model of geometric sans serifs has more to do with the success of its nearly identical copies in the United States than it does with its geometrical perfection; in Europe, Futura was never the only model and never the only market leader. Today the success of copies defines the aesthetic and cultural reach of the original. In fifty years, it is possible that the only version of Futura anyone will remember will be a free version on GitHub or Google Fonts. Appropriately enough, the only open-source Futura is named after its major American copy: Spartan. But then again, this copy will probably only do what every other copy has done: drive people back to the original.

Though any new creation loses Renner's hand or Bauer's machine precision, in an age of mass production, the model proves far more useful as a template than the original design. Tiny lead letters packed in heavy boxes and stored in orderly trays reach only as far as their modes of distribution. Futura is really more about a more far-reaching idea: a self-assured geometric sans serif, not too rigid but still precise, simplified forms thoughtfully stripped of extraneous complexity, a marriage of hand and machine. It is an aesthetic idea about modernity—clean lines with a slight human touch, embodied in a name filled with hope.

3

DEGENERATE TYPOGRAPHY

MOST TYPOGRAPHIC STYLES have long abandoned their youthful activism. Like responsible adults, they've put away their rally cries and found gainful employment. Typographic styles regain their political passion on occasion, but most typefaces, like most people, are not political extremists. Yet, because type is visible language, all politics is clothed in type. Political typographic styles shout slogans, rally voters, and fight political battles street by street, website by website, meme by meme.

In the United States, most campaigns are not sophisticated or centrally organized enough to apply the same typeface to all campaign materials. And yet political campaigns are all about controlling the message. Political signs of strength hinge on details: the number of supporters at a rally, the speed of sending out on-message tweets and emails, and the consistency of communication to supporters. Using the same typographic language in all these materials is one way to unify the message and forge a distinct voice.

PREVIOUS
1932 election poster for the Communist Party of Germany, designed with an early cut of Futura Bold with a long capital J

"Hitler! The faith and hope of millions!" German National Election handbill supporting the Nazi Party, typeset in blackletter, 1932

If you wanted to defeat Adolf Hitler in 1932, your vote might have been for Futura or, more precisely, the Communist Party candidate advertised using Futura. Posters proclaimed, "Fight against Hunger and War" or "Capitalism Robs You of the Last Piece of Bread," with each call to action printed in Futura Bold: vote Thälmann. Designed by the artist John Heartsfield for the campaign, most of the Communist campaign materials were set in Futura or similarly modern sans serifs like Kabel.[1]

In 1932 the German people had a difficult choice: vote for a Communist bent on revolution or for rightwing extremists bent on violent change. At stake were the 386 seats in the Reichstag (the German parliament) and the control of the republic. Voting was fierce, and the campaigns extended through every city and hamlet in the country. Posters, placards, and handbills were plastered on every available surface. On these walls and on the streets, the primary messages of a mass media campaign battled between Communists, Social Democrats, National Socialists, and other smaller parties, each brandishing propaganda with distinct color and typography to win converts to their cause.

The world now mourns the dire consequences of the 1932 election and Hitler's rise to power. In 1933 Hitler declared war on all art forms he disagreed with. Famously, as art director in chief of the German nation, he instituted a strict regimen of design for the Nazi Party, with a new logo, stark red and black colors stolen from the Communists (whose branding he saw as more effective than other parties'), and a new reliance on German-centric typography. With Hitler's rise, foundries released new modernist blackletters that have since been termed "jackboot" letters for their unambiguous

nationalism: Deutschland (Germany), Tannenburg (the name of a World War I German victory), and Adler (Eagle). As Hitler consolidated power, he used his cultural influence to push out those he considered undesirables. The Bauhaus closed, and many of its faculty and students moved abroad to the United States, the United Kingdom, Palestine, Brazil, Argentina, and elsewhere. While some worked with the regime, many were persecuted, imprisoned, or killed.[2]

Other schools were similarly purged. Jan Tschichold and Paul Renner were arrested and removed from their Munich-based design school, where Renner had served as director since 1927. Renner had helped design the German section at the Milan Triennale for the government in 1933, but was arrested for publishing an anti-Nazi pamphlet in 1932 called "Kulturbolschewismus?" ("Cultural Bolshevism?"), decrying the attempts by the Nazi state to influence culture and art.[3]

Starting in 1935, Hitler's government staged a now infamous art show called Entartete Kunst (Degenerate Art) that set up for ridicule many modern artists

In 1932 Hitler's political team used whatever types they could to win. Many of his party's election posters featured blackletter types. Yet one of his posters was the most minimal of the election (above right).

Adlerwerke
Gotenburg
Tannenburg

DEGENERATE TYPOGRAPHY 67

The multiparty election of 1932 was, in part, a circular firing squad of party against party. Above, the Social Democrats poster is "Against Papen, Hitler, Thälmann."

who would later become famous, including Wassily Kandinsky, Paul Klee, Emil Nolde, and Otto Dix. The show displayed the works haphazardly, with annotated blackletter wall graphics lampooning the work.

In the process of advertising for the event, modern typography was targeted as well. One of the main posters for Entartete Kunst in Berlin used several weights of Futura, associating, through the layout itself, new typography with the culturally condemned modern art. Of course, type is not so monolithic or partisan; Hitler's Germany put on a good face for the 1936 Olympics, casting Futura to play a starring role in its signage and documents. Futura promoted the nation in signage at the German exhibit at the international exhibit of Barcelona—for good reason too. Before Entartete Kunst and Hitler's rise to power, Futura had enjoyed

 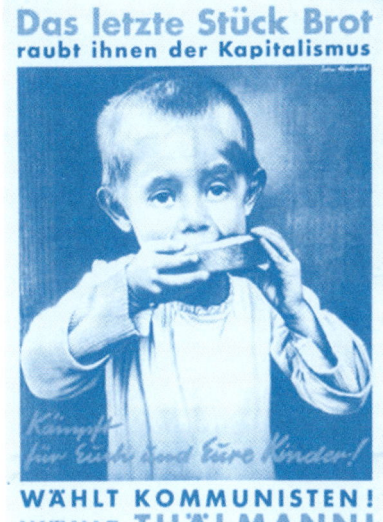

1932 national election posters for Adolf Hitler, leader of the Nazi Party (left), and for Ernst Thälmann, the leader of the Communists (right)

widespread adoption by printers, mapmakers, and advertisers throughout Germany. Most famously, the city of Hannover rebranded all its official documentation to be set in Futura.[4] Corporations all across the country used Futura to sell their wares, package their products, and print their books.

Outside of Germany in the 1930s, Futura and its modernist brothers were the face of a new international typography. These typefaces and new designers coming from Germany were harbingers of a new style emerging from the Continent, even while the Nazi Party was internally propagating a far more nationalistic and inward-looking type design.

The Nazi party, however, was ruthlessly pragmatic in its use of type. As Germany conquered neighboring countries, it was faced with a dilemma: while

DEGENERATE TYPOGRAPHY

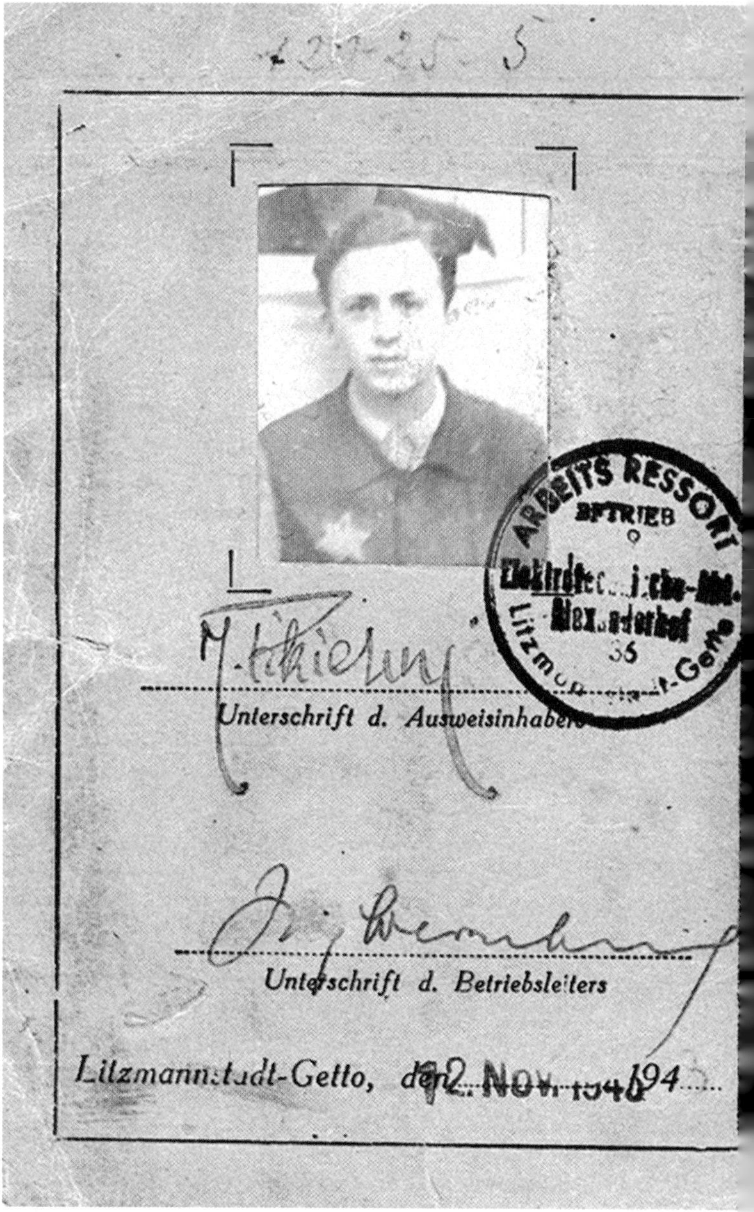

Unterschrift d. Ausweisinhabers

Unterschrift d. Betriebsleiters

Litzmannstadt-Getto, den 194

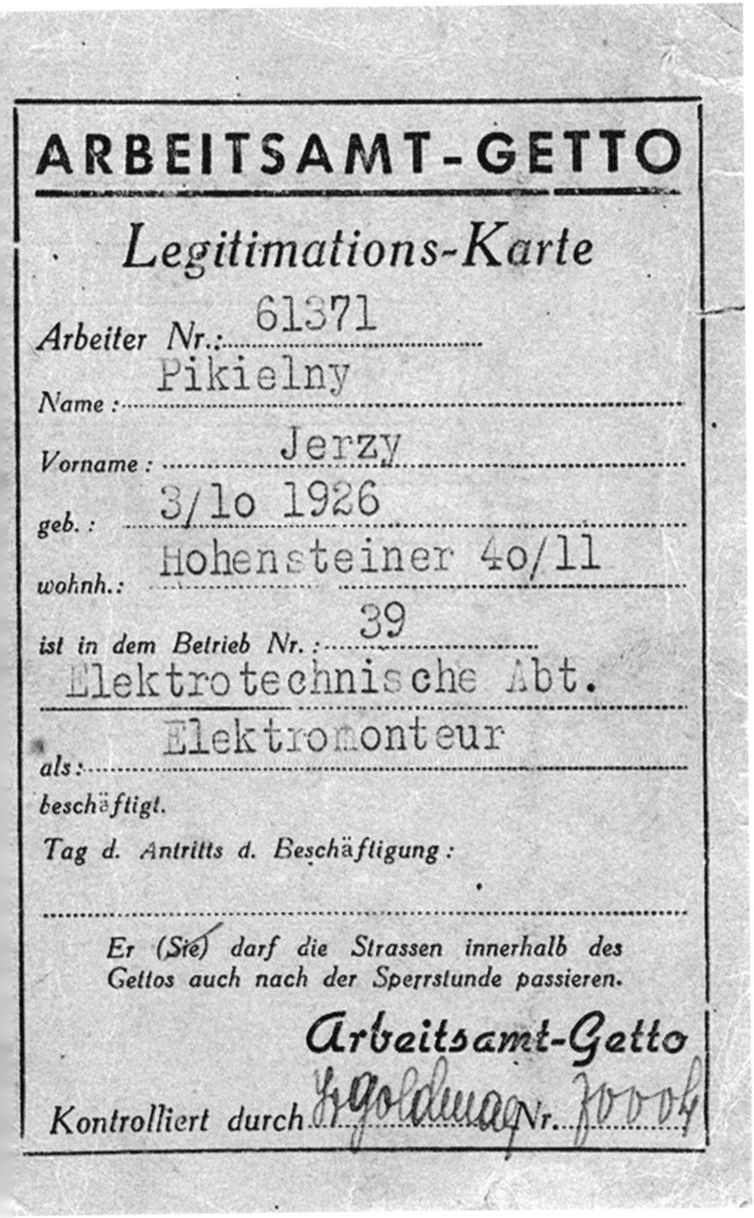

ARBEITSAMT-GETTO

Legitimations-Karte

Arbeiter Nr.: 61371

Name: Pikielny

Vorname: Jerzy

geb.: 3/1o 1926

wohnh.: Hohensteiner 4o/11

ist in dem Betrieb Nr.: 39

Elektrotechnische Abt.

als: Elektromonteur

beschäftigt.

Tag d. Antritts d. Beschäftigung:

Er (Sie) darf die Strassen innerhalb des Gettos auch nach der Sperrstunde passieren.

Arbeitsamt-Getto

Kontrolliert durch *H.Goldman* Nr. *10004*

PREVIOUS
Work-camp permits for Jews and other political prisoners used Futura and other sans serifs after a 1941 decree branded German blackletter Jewish.

John Heartfield used Futura to complement his biting photomontages in *Arbeiter-Illustrierte-Zeitung* or *AIZ* (the *Workers Pictorial Newspaper*), a German magazine published between 1924 and 1933.

blackletter was easy for Germans to understand, it adapted poorly to other languages, and other countries did not have enough blackletter type to print all their official documents. In 1941, at the height of the Nazi empire (which by then had taken over France, Belgium, Ukraine, Czechoslovakia, and Poland), the government issued an abrupt, if not problematic, message of its own, signaling a deeply cynical about-face on policy: henceforth, the Nazi government would no longer use blackletter, having discovered that it was actually Jewish in origin and not German. Roman typefaces would now reign across the empire. In its darkest incarnation, this policy change can be

seen in prisoners' work permits, including those for Jews in ghettos throughout Poland and Ukraine. In the permits issued in 1939, the titles were set in blackletter. From 1941 and onward, they were set in sans serifs, many in Futura.[5]

In other contexts, Futura was less partisan but still political. In the United States, where Futura became an almost overnight hit, it was so widely used that it never had time to acquire a partisan tinge. Even while some American printers and typographers decried the modernist changes in orthography, like lowercase letters and new typography styles, most attempts to connect type with ideology were satirized and rejected. Instead, for most of the war and most of the twentieth century, Futura enjoyed broad currency across the political spectrum.

When the United States entered World War II in 1941, government printers used Spartan, a Futura clone, on many of the country's maps and as the official footer on its propaganda posters. Starting with the candidacy of war hero Dwight D. Eisenhower, every campaign for the next two decades (until Richard Nixon) featured Futura in some way, on buttons, posters, flyers, or other ephemera. But this doesn't mean that there was some grand design: for the most part, American political designs were not that sophisticated. Everyone printed with the same typefaces as a matter of custom and habit. Democrats and Republicans advertised in both red and blue, using largely the same handful of typefaces: Franklin Gothic, Futura, and whatever else the local printer had on hand. This reflected not a political fascination with Futura, but rather the cultural dominance of Futura as an advertising and commercial typeface, which made it a clear choice for campaigns as well.

One of several infamous Degenerate Art show posters. The poster uses Futura Bold and Futura Black for all of the smaller type. The title is hand-lettered but is styled after modernist types.

By 1972, however, campaigns had started to become more deliberate in their branding and design. Nixon's reelection campaign used Futura, perhaps because it was similar to election materials he had used as Eisenhower's running mate, two decades earlier, or perhaps because a consultant discovered that a rounder typeface might make a somewhat unlikable president seem friendlier and more of the people. With it came the slogan "President Nixon. Now more than ever," in a comprehensive program of identity design that would not be equaled by any presidential candidate until Barack Obama's 2008 campaign. To read Nixon's campaign brochures today is to receive a shock: Republicans for health care, environmental protection, and federal education policy. Maybe Futura has always been to the left of certain ideologies. Nixon's 1972 reelection campaign was a dramatic success, but was ultimately discredited by scandal and dishonesty. Nixon resigned in 1974.

The UK Conservative Party campaigned with Futura leading up to the 2015 election.

Ronald Reagan's successful use of Garamond, and Nixon's failure with Futura, ensured that hundreds of down-ballot politicians followed suit. Politicians don't really care about typography itself—they use what wins. In the United States, at least, after the 2008 triumph of Obama and the widespread association of his campaign with Gotham, geometric sans serifs like Gotham proliferated in campaigns throughout America. Across the ocean in the United Kingdom, possibly looking to assume a more forward-thinking mantle, David Cameron and the UK Conservative Party used Futura for nearly all campaign materials during 2014 election.

In the United Kingdom the use of Futura was a surprise twist, given that Futura was largely eclipsed in the twentieth century by Gill Sans, a modernist typeface with decidedly English roots. Labour's 1945 parliamentary

Mirroring sophisticated corporate brands, Richard Nixon used Futura almost exclusively for his 1972 reelection campaign materials, unlike previous politicians.

Futura, employed by dozens of workaday printers to create simple American election materials. It was used by both parties throughout the midcentury: Dwight D. Eisenhower vs. Aldai E. Stevenson (1952 and 1956), Nixon vs. John F. Kennedy (1960), and Lyndon B. Johnson vs. Barry Goldwater (1964).

victory was built, in part, on posters designed with Gill Sans, including one that read, "AND NOW—WIN THE PEACE, VOTE LABOUR," featuring a giant sans serif *V* towering over the countryside. And Conservatives regained the government in 1950 campaigning with dozens of different posters nationwide, all incorporating a cohesive design that included Gill Sans. Later campaigns in the 1960s introduced Franklin Gothic and other sans serifs into British politics, but it was not until the 1970s that Futura was employed—with limited use in the 1974 Conservative campaign and extensive use in Conservative candidates' posters for the 1979 inaugural European Parliament elections.

In contrast to the ever-changing styles and preferences of American political parties, the Social Democratic Party of Germany (SPD) has used Futura consistently for its logo since well before the Berlin Wall fell. The three letters *S*, *P*, and *D* in white on a red square are as recognizable for the SPD and are as dominant as the party's electoral success for over thirty years. And yet, even in Germany, Futura is the typeface of aspirants: the major left-wing parties, Die Linke (literally, "the Left," formed in 2007) and Bündnis 90/Die Grünen (a merger of the Green Party and Alliance '90), have both set their logos in Futura Bold Condensed Oblique. And in 2013, following a similar rise of far-right parties across Europe, a new anti-immigrant, nationalistic party was formed: Alternative für Deutschland (AFD). AFD uses Futura for all its materials, perhaps as a way to convey instant familiarity and attempt to signal forward-looking, modern views, despite its reactionary politics.

In any election, type matters. In 2012 Democratic president Obama's campaign commissioned a variant

In 2017 four German political parties use Futura: the Social Democratic Party, Die Linke, Bündnis 90/Die Grünen, and Alternative für Deutschland.

"And Now—Win the Peace, Vote Labor" UK election poster, 1945

"Vote Conservative" UK election posters, 1950

2012 US presidential candidate Mitt Romney used Trajan for his campaign logo.

of Gotham, his successful 2008 campaign typeface designed by Hoefler & Frere-Jones. The new typeface, Gotham Slab, cemented Obama's reputation for cutting-edge design but was still familiar enough to be reassuring. Republican candidate Mitt Romney went with Trajan, a decidedly conservative typeface—perhaps "severely conservative," as Romney called himself.[6] Trajan is based on centuries-old Roman inscriptions and is ubiquitous in contemporary university branding and film posters, making the choice both generic and safe.[7] Signs used at Romney rallies, however, featured the much more contemporary typefaces Mercury and Whitney, which were also designed by Hoefler & Frere-Jones, making the use of typefaces from the firm a rare point of bipartisanship.

After using Gotham for much of the 2008 campaign, Barack Obama's 2012 reelection team commissioned Gotham Slab from Jonathan Hoefler and Tobias Frere-Jones.

WESTERN DEFENSE COMMAND AND FOURTH ARMY
WARTIME CIVIL CONTROL ADMINISTRATION

Presidio of San Francisco, California
April 1, 1942

INSTRUCTIONS TO ALL PERSONS OF JAPANESE ANCESTRY

Living in the Following Area:

All that portion of the City and County of San Francisco, State of California, lying generally west of the north-south line established by Junipero Serra Boulevard, Worchester Avenue, and Nineteenth Avenue, and lying generally north of the east-west line established by California Street, to the intersection of Market Street, and thence on Market Street to San Francisco Bay.

All Japanese persons, both alien and non-alien, will be evacuated from the above designated area by 12:00 o'clock noon Tuesday, April 7, 1942.

No Japanese person will be permitted to enter or leave the above described area after 8:00 a. m., Thursday, April 2, 1942, without obtaining special permission from the Provost Marshal at the Civil Control Station located at:

> 1701 Van Ness Avenue
> San Francisco, California

The Civil Control Station is equipped to assist the Japanese population affected by this evacuation in the following ways:

1. Give advice and instructions on the evacuation.
2. Provide services with respect to the management, leasing, sale, storage or other disposition of most kinds of property including: real estate, business and professional equipment, buildings, household goods, boats, automobiles, livestock, etc.
3. Provide temporary residence elsewhere for all Japanese in family groups.
4. Transport persons and a limited amount of clothing and equipment to their new residence, as specified below.

The Following Instructions Must Be Observed:

1. A responsible member of each family, preferably the head of the family, or the person in whose name most of the property is held, and each individual living alone, will report to the Civil Control Station to receive further instructions. This must be done between 8:00 a. m. and 5:00 p. m., Thursday, April 2, 1942, or between 8:00 a. m. and 5:00 p.m., Friday, April 3, 1942.

2. Evacuees must carry with them on departure for the Reception Center, the following property:
   (a) Bedding and linens (no mattress) for each member of the family;
   (b) Toilet articles for each member of the family;
   (c) Extra clothing for each member of the family;
   (d) Sufficient knives, forks, spoons, plates, bowls and cups for each member of the family;
   (e) Essential personal effects for each member of the family.

All items carried will be securely packaged, tied and plainly marked with the name of the owner and numbered in accordance with instructions received at the Civil Control Station.

The size and number of packages is limited to that which can be carried by the individual or family group.

No contraband items as described in paragraph 6, Public Proclamation No. 3, Headquarters Western Defense Command and Fourth Army, dated March 24, 1942, will be carried.

3. The United States Government through its agencies will provide for the storage at the sole risk of the owner of the more substantial household items, such as iceboxes, washing machines, pianos and other heavy furniture. Cooking utensils and other small items will be accepted if crated, packed and plainly marked with the name and address of the owner. Only one name and address will be used by a given family.

4. Each family, and individual living alone, will be furnished transportation to the Reception Center. Private means of transportation will not be utilized. All instructions pertaining to the movement will be obtained at the Civil Control Station.

Go to the Civil Control Station at 1701 Van Ness Avenue, San Francisco, California, between 8:00 a. m. and 5:00 p. m., Thursday, April 2, 1942, or between 8:00 a. m. and 5:00 p. m., Friday, April 3, 1942, to receive further instructions.

> J. L. DeWITT
> Lieutenant General, U. S. Army
> Commanding

SEE CIVILIAN EXCLUSION ORDER NO. 5

Civilian Exlcusion Order No. 1, April 1, 1942, posted to announce internment of Japanese American citizens during World War II, printed in California in Futura (or Spartan?)

just before the flag reaches the point opposite you and hold the salute until it has passed. When you pass the flag, come to salute six steps before you reach it and hold the salute until you are six steps past. In formation, you salute at command of your leader.

When the flag is carried, there should be an honor guard on each side of it. When carried with other flags, the flag should be in front of the others, or to the right if the flags are arranged in line. The flag of the United States is never dipped in salute to any person or thing.

Displaying the Flag. There is a right and a wrong way to display the flag, whether on the wall or from a staff. You should know the right way—and you should also know that the flag is never used as drapery (use red, white, and blue bunting instead); that nothing is ever placed on it; and that it never touches the ground, the floor, or water beneath it.

When the flag passes you, come to attention and salute it.

Below: In line with other flags, U.S. flag goes to its own right. It is always hoisted first and lowered last. Hoisted with another flag — troop, city, or state — U.S. flag is at the peak.

Futura was often used in conjunction with similar typefaces in different sizes, especially in encyclopedias, and manuals. In the case of the Boy Scouts of America's 1965 *Boy Scout Handbook,* Futura or Spartan is paired with Intertype Vogue (see chapter 2).

The use of new geometric typefaces for political campaigns is not limited to the national scale. My grandpa used ITC Avant Garde and Helvetica in his campaign to run as county commissioner in Provo, Utah, in 1974.

In the 2016 US presidential campaign, Hillary Clinton ditched the Reaganesque Garamond Bold (used for her senate races in 2000 and 2006, as well as her 2008 presidential bid) in favor of a forward-looking custom version of Sharp Sans, which in turn was modeled on Futura. At the campaign's request, the new font was named Unity—no doubt in hope of inspiring consistent use across her campaign, but also a foretasting of a larger political agenda.

"Hillary Clinton for US Senate" poster, 2000

This attention to typography reveals a deeper truth about the candidate and her team. Using a Futura-based typeface speaks to a desire for friendliness: the campaign material was largely printed in upper- and lowercase, showing off the typeface's approachable, round shapes. Even the rounded dots on the *i* and *j* were specially commissioned, to complete the look. Their consistent use of Unity demonstrated a concern about details, people, and policy. On this point, the mode of delivery matched the message: clean typography could unify the campaign and win over undecided voters.[8]

On the Republican side of the 2016 campaign, various candidates used Futura or Futura-like typefaces in their campaigns: Chris Christie, Marco Rubio, and Jeb Bush. (If you look past the exclamation point logo, most of the latter's posters and materials were set in Futura.) The broad similarity in campaign designs, especially on social media, may have contributed to the inability of each of the candidates to convince Americans of the uniqueness of his or her messages, and demonstrates that campaign design follows trends more often than it sets them. Perhaps each candidate wanted to fit in rather than stand out.

The one Republican candidate who did stand out, Donald Trump, seemed to care less about the mode of

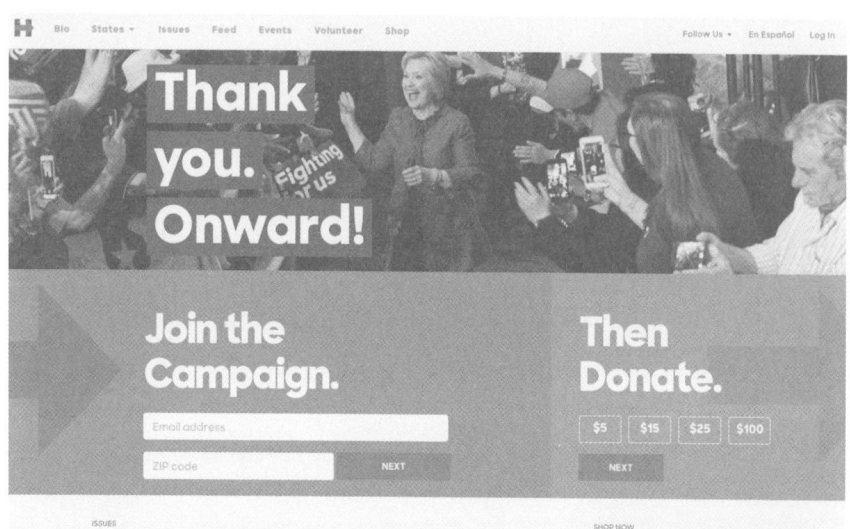

TOP Hillary Clinton used Unity, a custom version of Sharp Sans, for her website and campaign materials in 2016.

ABOVE Sharp Sans is a 2013 typeface by Lucas Sharp, a Brooklyn-based type designer (see chapter 8).

TOP Donald Trump's most memorable piece of campaign promotion was his red Make America Great Again hat. Worn by supporters throughout the 2016 presidential race, the simple, almost undesigned hat epitomized the campaign's antiestablishment, anti-elite message.

ABOVE In 2016 Trump's team relied on state party officials to create their own materials. Many states chose their own typefaces to make official Trump signs. CLOCKWISE FROM TOP LEFT: Provo, Utah; Phoenix, Arizona; Las Vegas, Nevada; Charlottesville, Virginia.

DEGENERATE TYPOGRAPHY

Many 2016 Republican presidential candidates used Futura in their campaigns, including Jeb Bush (right), John Kasisch, and Marco Rubio (opposite), even if they didn't use it for their official logo. Rubio used Avant Garde, a 1970s take on Futura.

communication than the result itself. His campaign's typography was loud and inconsistent (appearing in official capacities in multiple typefaces) or, alternatively, depending on your point of view, direct, bold, and forthright. While designs and typesetting varied from state to state, and even county to county, the giant white letters **TRUMP** were set most often in Akzidenz-Grotesk Bold Extended, but also sometimes in the Microsoft and Google Docs default, Arial. The official slogan under his name was typeset in Meta, a typeface popularized in American businesses in the late 1980s and early '90s (when Trump made his fortune). Trump's most memorable piece of campaign propaganda was not a sign, however, but a hat, emblazoned with the phrase "Make America Great Again." The phrase was typeset in Times New Roman—a choice that was almost an antichoice, as Times New Roman is a default for many systems (including Microsoft Word). In a way, the design of his products, like his campaign itself, championed the American proletariat voter against snobbish elitism.[9]

Clinton's design worked to win her the national vote; Trump's campaign (and design) was less popular overall. But for disaffected voters in many key states, Trump himself was the ultimate brand. His personal voice demanding change, for good and ill,

was ubiquitous during the campaign, with numerous television appearances, press conferences instead of interviews, and a personal Twitter account that became a particular source of controversy—in part for retweeting dubious news stories, appropriating memes with racist or xenophobic origins—but above all for Trump's personal tweets at all hours. For Clinton, all the professionalism, ground gaming, data crunching, and clever typography in the world wasn't enough. America's Electoral College system enabled white rural voters to propel Trump to victory, even though they represented less than half the popular vote.

In these contexts, designing slogans in one typeface or another acquires specific meaning. In a convention hall or on a street corner, the color and typeface might be all you see as a voter to understand that the candidate is speaking to you, and the way you understand that message might be the only thing to help you decide on your vote. In the early days of Futura, that choice appeared stark for some: choose Futura or choose Hitler. Today, in our vastly more commercial sphere, typefaces are more prevalent than ever. Used in thousands of contexts, the distinctions between campaigns seem less obvious. But if you look closely, the distinctions appear as essential and effective as ever.

4

OVER THE MOON FOR FUTURA

STANLEY KUBRICK'S 1968 FILM has one of the most iconic openings in history. A clarion trumpet heralds the first composed image: the earth, and the distant, much smaller sun, rising over the surface of the moon, all seen from a distant vantage point in space. The sun soars over the earth to perfect view in glorious symmetry with the thin geometric sans serif title: 2OO1: A SPACE ODYSSEY. The precise geometry of round Os notwithstanding, the type is not Futura, though the title is meant to look like it. Instead, the film's designers used Gill Sans and replaced the traditional oval-shaped zeros (0) with round Os, a hallmark of Futura—a typeface whose sleek geometric shapes and pure reduction of form helped pioneer modernism in typography.

In a dramatic echo, one year later and with the entire world watching, astronauts left these words on a plaque on the moon set in Futura:
HERE MEN FROM THE PLANET EARTH
FIRST SET FOOT UPON THE MOON
JULY 1969, A. D.
WE CAME IN PEACE FOR ALL MANKIND

Futura was used extensively in advertising for the 1968 film *2001: A Space Odyssey*, but sparingly in the film itself.

NASA employed Futura quite often, including in the patch for the first successful moon-landing mission, Apollo 11, in 1969.

It seems simple and appropriate that the plaque commemorating the moon landing is set in Futura; today many designers search magazines, design blogs, movies, and other media for inspiration, and in 1969, *2001* and its science-fiction siblings still largely defined images of space travel, cosmic intelligence, and scientific knowledge for astronaut and public alike.[1] You can almost imagine a NASA designer culling images of *2001* trailers and marketing material, looking for the perfect design for the plaque that would define the United States' mission in space for decades to follow.

Yet the reality of why Futura was chosen for the moon plaque is both mundane and deeply consequential. As important as the plaque was, Futura had been chosen long beforehand, not by a scheming designer, but by committees of government practitioners armed with the need for a clear, universally available default typeface. NASA contracted out all the work for the different components of the Apollo spacecraft and then adopted them into the agency's own system, partially by stamping controls, supplies, and manuals with its own labels. Most of these were set in Futura (or its clone, Spartan). As a result, Futura was used at every important moment of the Apollo missions, the heart of NASA's space program from 1967 to 1972.

The Apollo missions embody the power of clear communication and interlocking systems. Systems are processes and interactions that have been formalized into rules or standards. Once those standards have been adopted, they mobilize incredible power. The most iconic manifestation of the system is the countdown checklist operation. A representative for each mechanical and electric component of a space-bound rocket is required to give a positive word before the thrilling proclamation of "All systems go—proceed with operation" that precedes a countdown and launch. It is a system that formalizes and simplifies the thinking of the thousands of people working on the rockets. In optimized systems, all the people involved contribute to their fullest, knowing that their individual work is essential to the whole—and that they do not have to understand the whole in order for it to work. The checklist process was just one of many essential parts of the mechanisms for communication in the NASA system.

So why and how did Futura become the visual moniker of NASA's space systems, and why was it so pervasive? The components of the Apollo missions were designed and manufactured by hundreds of different contractors. For example, the medium-format camera that the Apollo 11 astronauts used to take pictures of the moon is a modified version of the Swedish Hasselblad 500EL camera, with special lubricants and coatings for use in space.[2] The lens dials and camera controls came to NASA with their traditional machine-routed type, just as the commercial versions had. However, on top of each NASA-use camera is a label with revised operating instructions set in Futura.

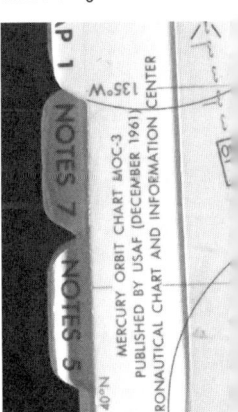

Since at least 1961, NASA has used Futura for its charts and manuals, including this one that John Glenn used while orbiting Earth.

The Futura sticker example typifies a practice that NASA engineers and builders repeated hundreds of times. By this process, Futura became ubiquitous within the compact space of 1960s-era spacecraft. The text on nearly every control in the command modules was set in Futura. Black type on silver adhesive labels marked daily food rations, tool bags, and even human-waste containers. Training and operating manuals primarily featured Futura; its presence served as evidence that an object had been vetted and cleared for use in the NASA system—both on the ground at mission control

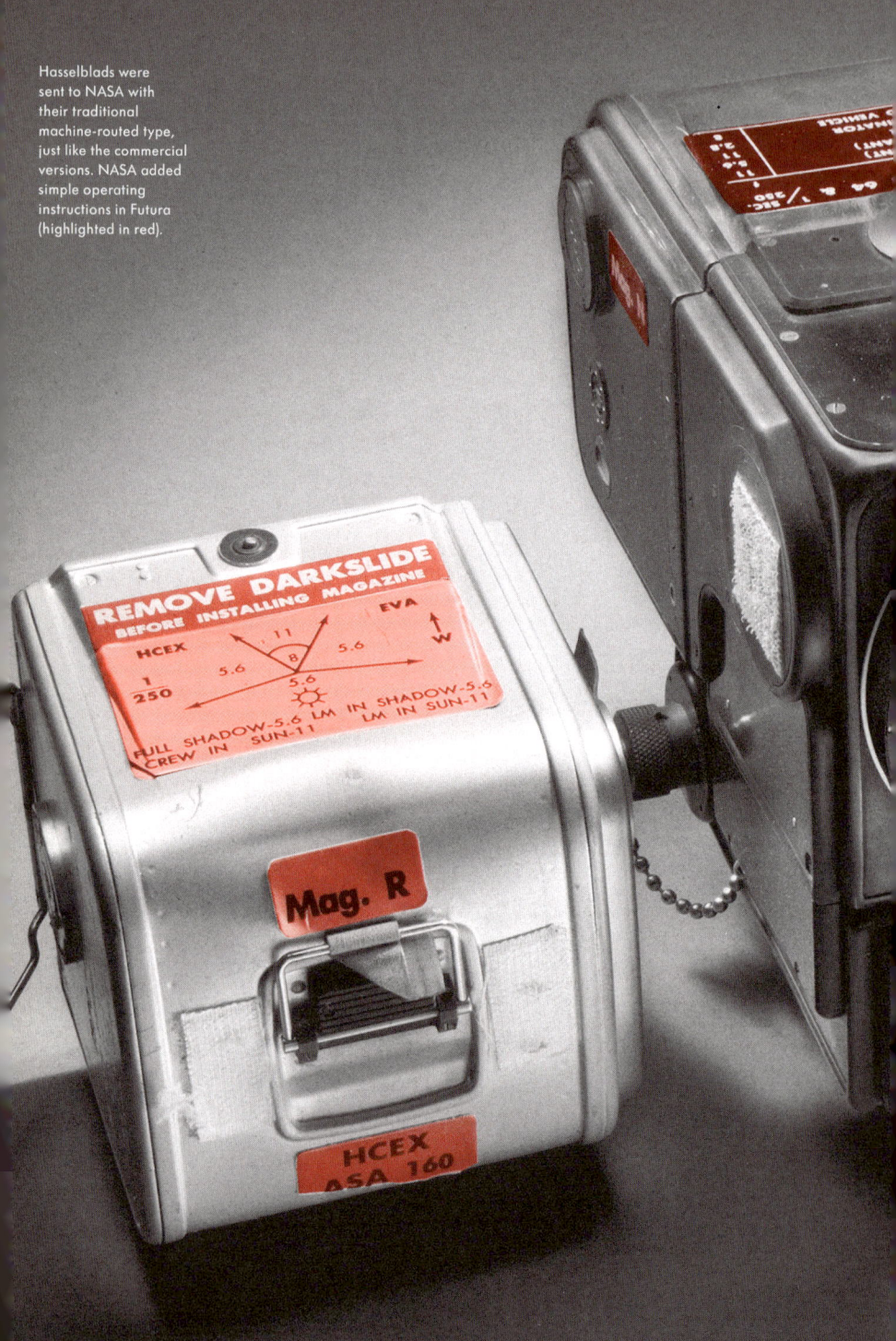

Hasselblads were sent to NASA with their traditional machine-routed type, just like the commercial versions. NASA added simple operating instructions in Futura (highlighted in red).

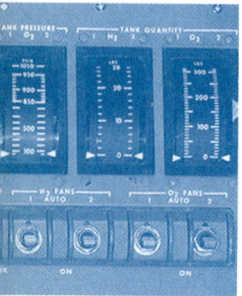

Futura was the primary typeface for the interfaces used by astronauts in the Apollo missions.

and in the spacecraft. The marking system legitimated each piece and, because of the visual similarity of each essential marking, contributed to ease of use.

Futura unified the components of the system. In a larger sense, the system is the way thousands of scientists, employees, and contractors worked together; for the astronauts, the system manifested itself on the instruments and supplies they took to the moon. Futura labels were intended primarily for them—the labels contained the most basic information the astronauts needed to know in order to use that device. There were other typefaces used, like those on the original labels that were part of the camera, but the point was to eliminate extraneous information. The astronauts had enough to worry about in space. So instead of asking them to master the various subtleties of operating one of the most complex and powerful cameras, NASA printed a label with simplified instructions. The fact that the label was printed in Futura made it part of a system that the astronauts easily recognized as their own. All the things they needed to know came from NASA, and all the things that came from NASA were written in Futura.

As the NASA model and thousands of other branding systems signal, the use of a specific typeface and style establishes authority and legitimacy for its users. This legitimacy, born of being recognizable, helps make systems work. For example, try downloading free software from today's internet. It's easy to get lost. The real download button jockeys with images, advertisements, and downloads for competing products. Many people never find it or hit the wrong button. It doesn't matter how well the software actually works—internet users afraid of downloading malware will try to seek

Futura legitimized most objects in the Apollo 11 system, including labels for daily meal packets and toolkits.

out the button that looks like it comes from a trusted source. Similarly, for the Apollo astronauts, knowing what every object was, and what do with it, was critical. Futura meant that the component had been vetted and approved.

Futura was one of the most visual manifestations of NASA's complex system working in harmony. Mission charts and maps set in Futura directed John Glenn as he first orbited the earth. Camera instructions in Futura coached Buzz Aldrin as he filmed Neil Armstrong taking the first step on the moon. After oxygen tanks exploded on Apollo 13, Jack Swigert watched plunging oxygen levels on indicator dials, each set in Futura. And after every successful mission, Futura-lettered labels on doors, levers, and knobs guided astronauts as they opened the hatches back on Earth, triumphant in their accomplishments.

The choice of Futura as the system typeface for the Apollo missions becomes clear once you imagine alternatives. The command module could have looked like a modern living room with its tangle of electronics—and been just as confusing. Imagine trying to remember, while hurtling into space, that your Sony remote connects to your Panasonic TV.

The choice of Futura wasn't necessarily a grand aesthetic statement of modernism unique to NASA and its space travel. Even though Futura had helped usher in American modernism in the 1930s and '40s, by the time of the Apollo program in the 1960s, it had become a generic choice. Futura (and its clones) was available from every typesetter and printer, and it was very popular in advertising, packaging, and labeling—including in the US military. The US Army had used Futura as the basis for its detailed global mapping project during

Futura and its competitors were well used in charts, maps, and diagrams throughout the postwar era in America.

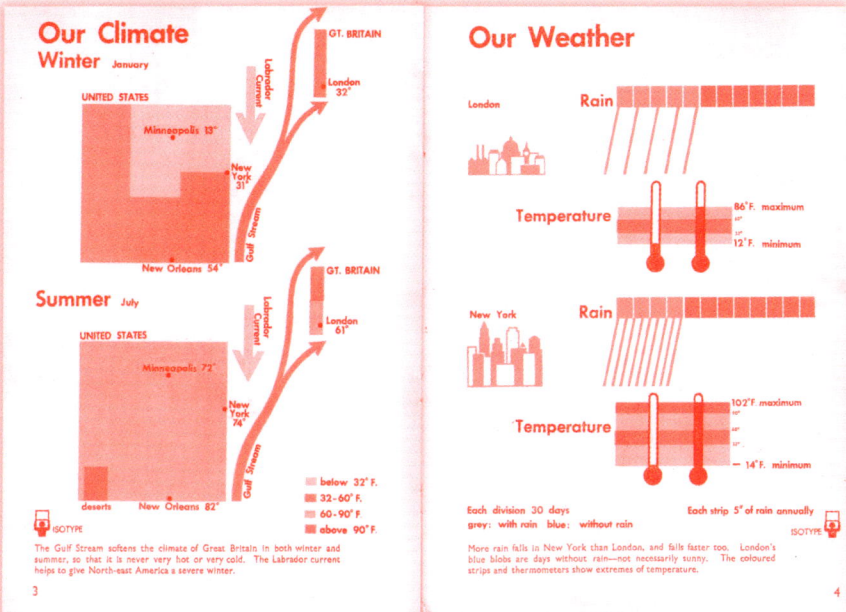

World War II, and the US Air Force had started using it on labels for its missiles by the late 1950s. By 1962 the typeface had been integrated into every chart created by air force printers for the Mercury space missions.[3] In 1969 Futura was part of default culture—present in every type case, font manual, and style guide in America—which arguably robbed it of its original modernist social message, as well as its avant-garde exclusivity.

Defaults are always conservative, because visual authority takes time to become established. In the 1920s and '30s, Futura was an insurgent type choice used by designers and advertisers to champion a new modernist look. By the 1950s and '60s, Futura (and its competitors) had become an established, authoritative label in charts and packaging because of the thou-

Otto Neurath pioneered a new system of graphically presenting statistical information. His company, ISOTYPE, used Futura almost exclusively to label the charts.

Futura found its way into dozens of federal logos, partially because it had acquired authority from other federal uses, but also because it was readily available.

OVER THE MOON FOR FUTURA   95

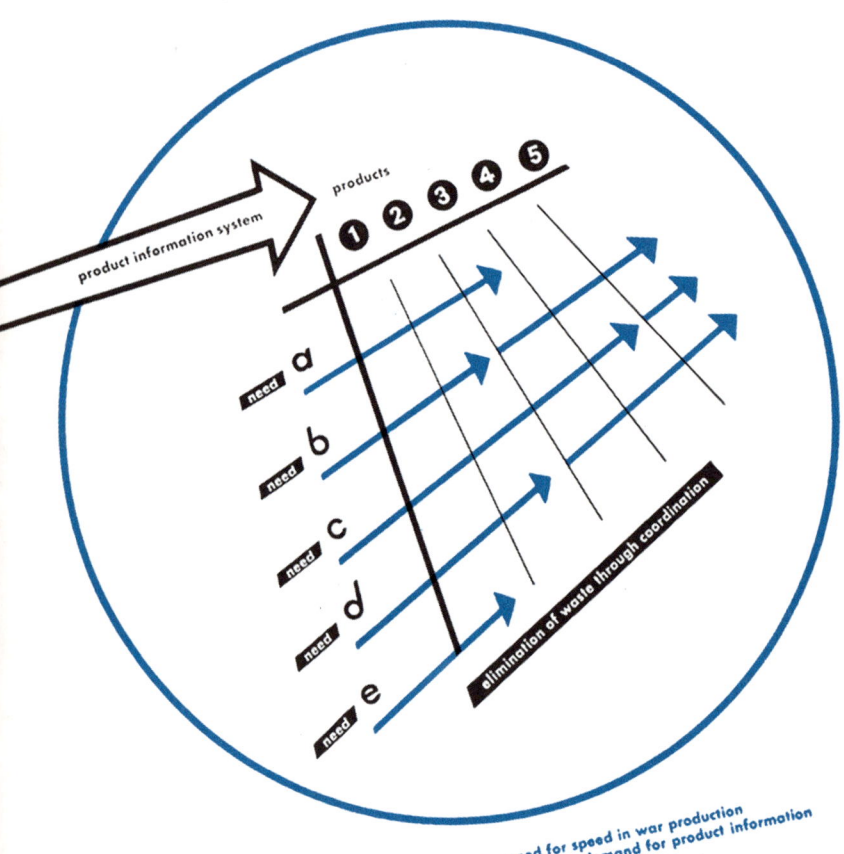

essential product information
accessible, up to date
eliminates waste, speeds production

the increasing need for speed in war production is reflected in increasing demand for product information

in order to be useful such product information should be comprehensive, concise, coordinated

prefiling of catalogs has been developed as a means for controlling the flow of essential product information

Sweet's Catalog Service
distribution - printing - design

The Czech exile Ladislav Sutnar helped pioneer information design and popularized Futura by using it in hundreds of charts and catalogs for American corporations as the chief designer at Sweet's Catalog Service. The above is an excerpt from Why, What, How, Essential Product Information, 1942.

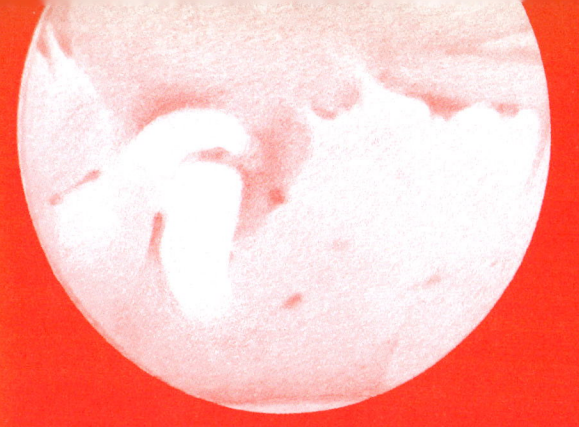
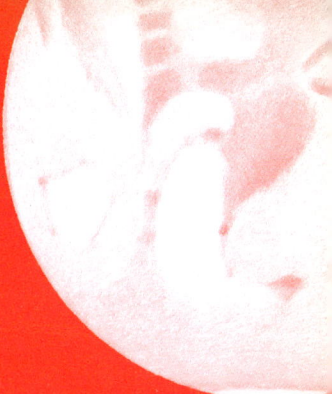

1 Winter: As Martian seasons change, astronomers can see marked changes taking place on planet. In these drawings notice how polar cap grows small as spring, early and late summer set in.

2 Spring: During spring gions near polar cap a equator begin to spre omers think that melt cap flows into areas

3 Early summer: By this time of the Martian year many canals bloom into sight. Some dark areas begin expanding at rate of 1 to 11 miles daily. Within weeks nearby land changes completely.

4 Late summer: Polar Canals become sharp a deep brown like fe the end of fall, brow fade and polar cap e

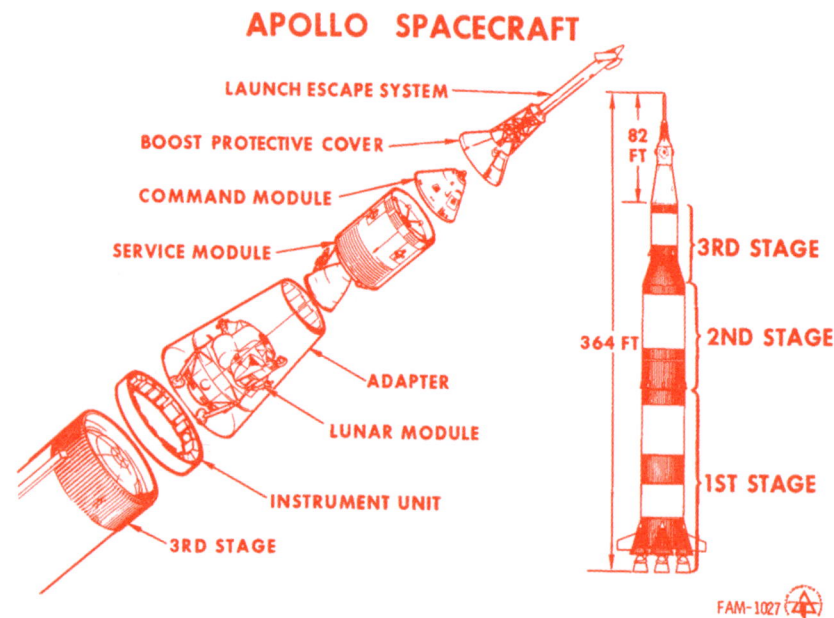

ABOVE NASA used Futura (or its copies) for most of the charts and diagrams used to train its astronauts until 1975.

PREVIOUS In the midcentury, Futura became popular for authoritative labels, including in Roy Gallant's *Exploring Mars*, 1956.

sands of schoolbooks, newspapers, encyclopedias, and magazines throughout America that had used it for headings, footnotes, and even the glance-only fine print of copyrights and publication dates. In these uses, Futura's authority drew power from its own ubiquity.

Over the last forty years, Helvetica has since taken on this mantle of ubiquity, becoming the typeface of choice for a variety of government and government-mandated publications, from tax documents to nutrition labels.[4] In 1976 NASA switched to Helvetica, under a new identity system designed by the firm Danne & Blackburn. The identity is associated with the famous "worm" logo, but its most lasting change was the adoption of Helvetica throughout the agency.[5] After 1976 NASA used Helvetica for its papers and publications as

Futura was well used in many publications—books, magazines, and encyclopedias—in the midcentury, including the 1955 book *Exploring the Moon*, designed by Alma Reese Cardi (left), and 1953's *World Geographic Atlas: A Composite of Man's Environment*, designed by Herbert Bayer and printed by Rand McNally (right).

well as all across the space program—including labels throughout the new space shuttles.[6]

NASA's use of Helvetica in 1976 wasn't any more avant-garde than its use of Futura a generation before—except as a signal that both typefaces had established themselves as defaults. But, where Futura emerged as a bureaucratic vernacular developed over decades, Helvetica was part of a full-fledged corporate identity program. The designers of the identity program mandated Helvetica, and NASA adopted it all at once.

By the late 1960s and throughout the 1970s, hundreds of corporations were choosing Helvetica in exactly the same way—accepting the wisdom of design firms to adopt new identity programs specifying the typeface. With overwhelming corporate adoption of

The NASA identity standards, created by design firm Danne & Blackburn in 1975, instituted Helvetica as the new primary typeface for all NASA materials.

OVER THE MOON FOR FUTURA   99

Helvetica, the typeface seems American in spite of its Swiss/German origins. In every year the space shuttle flew, it featured the words *United States* in Helvetica. And in 2016, unless you were a type nerd, when you saw Matt Damon try to survive a harsh alien planet in *The Martian*, you probably didn't even think about the type. Every supply crate and food ration labeled in Helvetica disappeared into the background because it had earned the power to do so, becoming tightly woven into the fabric of modern society.

Now that Futura is no longer this nation's default (and Helvetica and its clones are), Futura once again feels sexy, sleek, unique, and modern—far more than it did when it was used for the Apollo missions. In today's context, stripped of some of its everyday generic uses, Futura reacquires some of its original popularity: a perfect reduction of form and clean geometry that stands out as unique. In 1992 the former Soviet space program renamed itself as the Russian agency Roscosmos. As with many parts of the new Russian government, the agency wanted to project a new forward-looking image devoid of Soviet references. The logo, an upward red arrow reminiscent of the original NASA logo, was offset by a familiar typeface newly available in Cyrillic in 1991: Futura.

POCKOCMOC

In 1992 NASA reinstituted its original 1959 logo, but kept Helvetica as the default system typeface instead of reverting to Futura. In the same year, Russia's space agency, Roscosmos (Pockocmoc in Cyrillic), used Futura to accompany its logo.

The US armed forces made thousands of maps during World War II for use throughout the government. The typesetting did not start out consistent, but the maps evolved into a system with Futura as their mainstay typeface through the postwar era.

This map of Cuba from the Air Force was printed in 1962, one year after the failed US invasion and one year before the fateful Cuban Missile Crisis.

OPPOSITE This map of North Vietnam from the Army was printed in 1967, a year remembered primarily for the surprise counteroffensives of North Vietnam against US and South Vietnamese forces.

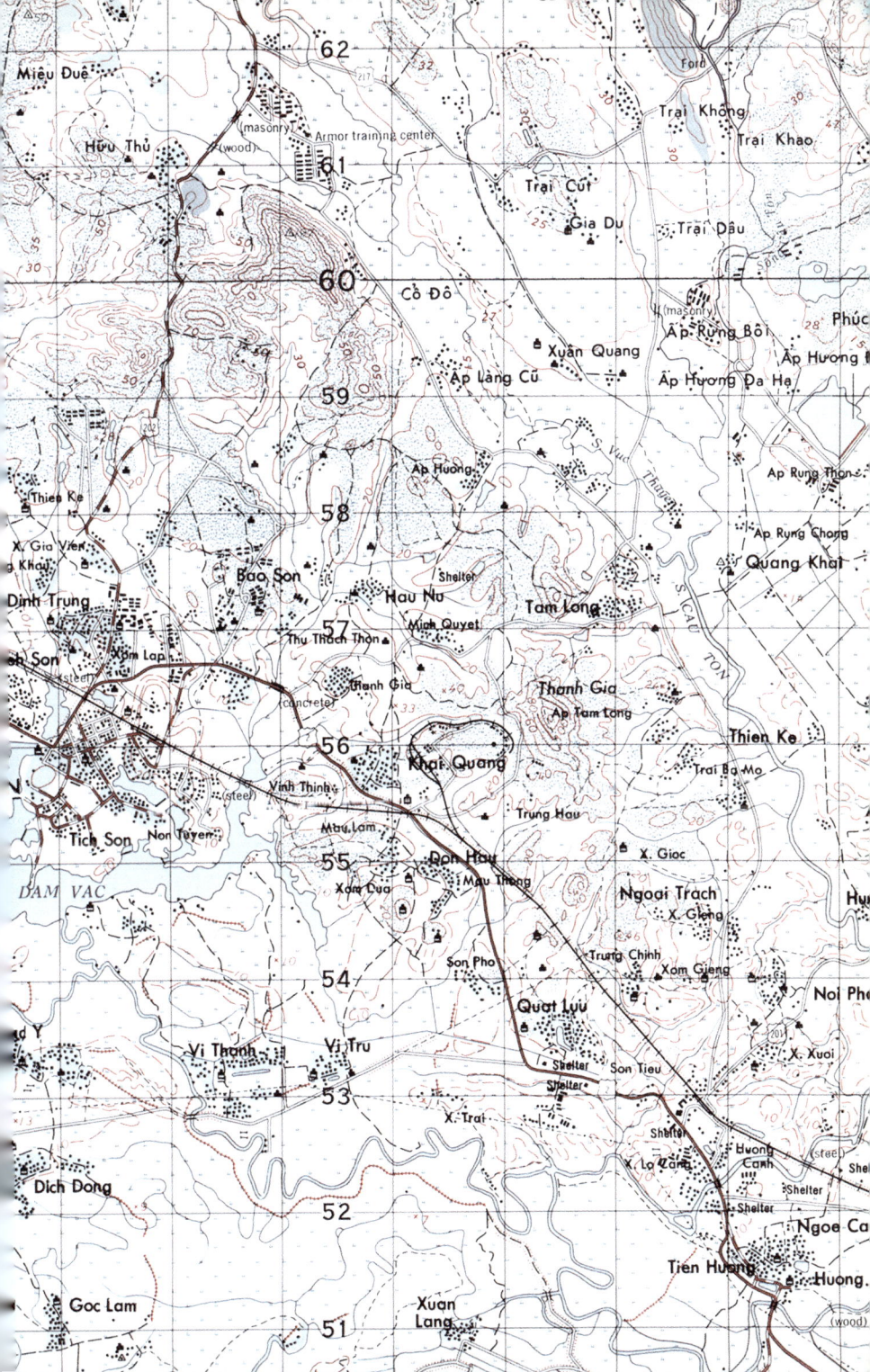

5

FUTURA IN THE WILD

DURING A LECTURE IN BALTIMORE introducing his latest typefaces, Christian Schwartz expressed a truth that every designer knows instinctually, even if he or she may not always want to believe it: "A typeface is not a magic bullet. The way it is used is critical."[1]

Typefaces are not typography: the space between letters or words or lines of type (kerning, tracking, and leading), not to mention text color, size, placement, and, above all, the negative space around text itself, combine to create the essential context in which a typeface is read. In part, this is what the designer Massimo Vignelli was getting at when he infamously declared that a designer only needs eight to twelve typefaces to complete a lifetime of work—and they should be a handful of classic, well-tested typefaces at that. For him, only through repeated use could a designer really discover all the true voices of a typeface, and become fluent in its particular needs and eccentricities.[2]

PREVIOUS
Futura can be found in diverse environments, including this electric pole in Harrington Park, New Jersey.

OPPOSITE
Adobe Futura might be the most common of all Futuras in the wild because it is bundled in Adobe's Creative Suite. Here is the full Adobe version of the family, excepting Futura Black.

Unsurprisingly, Vignelli's statement is mostly ignored and often criticized.[3] A glance at any shopping center or downtown plaza reveals dozens, if not hundreds, of unique typefaces. Even experienced designers search high and low to pair the perfect typeface with the perfect project. On a given job, he or she may go through hundreds of typefaces, hoping to find the one that creates a perfect synergy of medium and message, and project and client.

These practices notwithstanding, Vignelli is right about one thing, and no designer would directly criticize this idea: a typeface can speak in any number of voices depending on its use. There is no simple formula to dictate that henceforth and forever a typeface will be used and understood in a singular, specific way. Instead, typefaces, including Futura, take on different meanings for different people, in different contexts.

But this does not mean that Futura means everything all the time. In spite of our varied experiences and associations, certain products, industries, and ideas group around certain typefaces. In part because of its ubiquity and popularity, Futura is an easily tracked example of this phenomenon. This photo-essay tracks Futura in the wild, in one of its most natural habitats—semipermanent, street-level signage and its associated typography—becoming a cliché in certain industries and professions through repeated use.

Light

Light Oblique

Book

Book Oblique

Medium

Medium Oblique

Heavy

Heavy Oblique

Bold

Bold Oblique

Extra Bold

Extra Bold Oblique

Light Condensed

Light Condensed Oblique

Medium Condensed

Medium Condensed Oblique

Bold Condensed

Bold Condensed Oblique

Extra Bold Condensed

Extra Bold Condensed Oblique

IN THE MALL

Sleep Number — *Futura Light*

Forever 21 — *Futura Condensed*

Claire's — *Futura Bold*

Do lighter weights of Futura like Futura Medium signify more expensive goods?

Louis Vuitton — *Futura Medium (Twentieth Century)*

The Limited — *Futura Medium*

Dolce & Gabbana — *Futura Light*

ABOUT TOWN

Queen Elizabeth II Centre, London — *Futura Light*

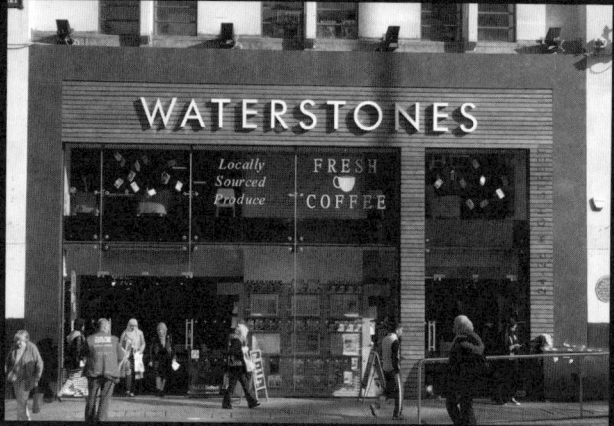

Waterstones, Birmingham, ENG — *Futura Light*

Apple Store Genius Bar, Towson, MD — *Futura Medium*

M Salon Federal Hill, Baltimore, MD *Futura Light*

The Temple salon, Frederick, MD *Futura Light*

Make Up For Ever, Dublin, IRL *Futura Medium*

BIG-BOX STORES

Many big-box stores in the United States use logos created from Futura and stretched for effect.

Bed Bath & Beyond — *Futura Light and Bold (stretched)*

Best Buy — *Futura Bold (stretched and rotated)*

Costco Wholesale — *Futura Bold Oblique*

PetSmart — *Futura Bold (on a curve)*

Big Lots — *Futura Extra Bold and Light*

Big Kmart — *Futura Extra Bold*

BIG-BOX STORES

DD's Discounts — *Futura Bold and Medium*

Shoppers World — *Futura Light and Extra Bold*

Aaron's — *Futura Bold Oblique*

EuroGiant — *Futura Bold (layered)*

Golf Galaxy — *Futura Bold (stretched and curved)*

Party City — *Futura Bold*

FOOD/OTHER

Geno's Steaks, Philadelphia — *Futura Extra Bold Condensed*

Collins Food, Baltimore, MD — *Futura Bold Condensed Italic*

Pi Pizza, Washington, DC — *Futura Bold*

Older neon signs rarely conform to a single typeface. This sign has letters based on Futura, like the C, but some individual letters have their own flair.

Baynesville Electronics, Towson, MD — *Custom*

One Penn Plaza, New York City — *Futura Medium*

KIPP, Washington, DC — *Futura Light*

CIVIC BUILDINGS

Fire Station — *Futura Bold*

Federal Building — *Futura Light*

Other sans serif signage is not a typeface at all, but custom-built lettering. These sturdy letters were built by the United Steel Workers of America Local 2610 in Dundalk, Baltimore.

United Steel Workers of America — *Custom*

Postal Service Vehicle Maintenance Facility — *Kabel*

Don't be fooled. Your local post office's sign might look like Futura, but it's not—it's probably Kabel, another German emigré type (see chapter 2).

Post Office — *Kabel*

Public Housing — *Futura Bold*

SIGNAGE

Dangerous Drop — *Futura Bold*

Fire Exit — *Futura Medium*

Beware of Dog — *Futura Condensed Bold Italic and Bold*

Caution Sign (on maintenance vehicle) *Futura Bold*

Caution: Automatic Door *Futura Bold*

Private Property *Futura Bold and Medium Oblique*

GAS/PETROL STATIONS

Marathon (USA) — *Futura Extra Bold*

Valero (Mexico + USA) — *Futura Extra Bold*

Maxol (Ireland) — *Futura Bold*

Lukoil (Russia + USA) — *Futura Bold*

Shell (Netherlands + USA) — *Futura Bold*

Although Shell stopped using Futura in its logo, it continues to use Futura for signage in all of its stations.

Liberty (USA) — *Futura Extra Bold*

Strangers ACN

ADOBE, 1987 Four weights are included with most Adobe products. Beware of older versions: the first digital ones featured an egg-shaped O. Linotype Futura is identical, with slightly adjusted spacing.

Strangers ACN

BITSTREAM, 1990–93 Features slightly squared-off curves, and shorter acenders and decenders. Among the earliest digital versions, this version is common in the wild.

Strangers ACN

URW, 1993 Features an extensive family with many weights, including small caps and the less common Futura Display, but not Futura Black.

Strangers ACN

URW NO. 2D, 1993 Created in partnership with Letraset. No. 2 is less extensive than URW Futura. Is favored by some designers setting text in smaller sizes (under 14 points).

Strangers ACN

PARATYPE FUTURIS, 1991 Originally created at ParaType (ParaGraph) by Vladimir Yefimov with Cyrillic characters. Condensed styles were added by in 1993 by Vladimir Yefimov and Alexander Tarbeev.

Strangers ACN

PARATYPE, 1995–98 Original Cyrillic styles created in 1995. Isabella Chaeva developed additional weights in 2007-09. The most common on the web in, thanks to its availability on Typekit since 2011.

Comparison of commerically available digital iterations of Futura in Medium weight at 32 points (right) and at 625 points (opposite)

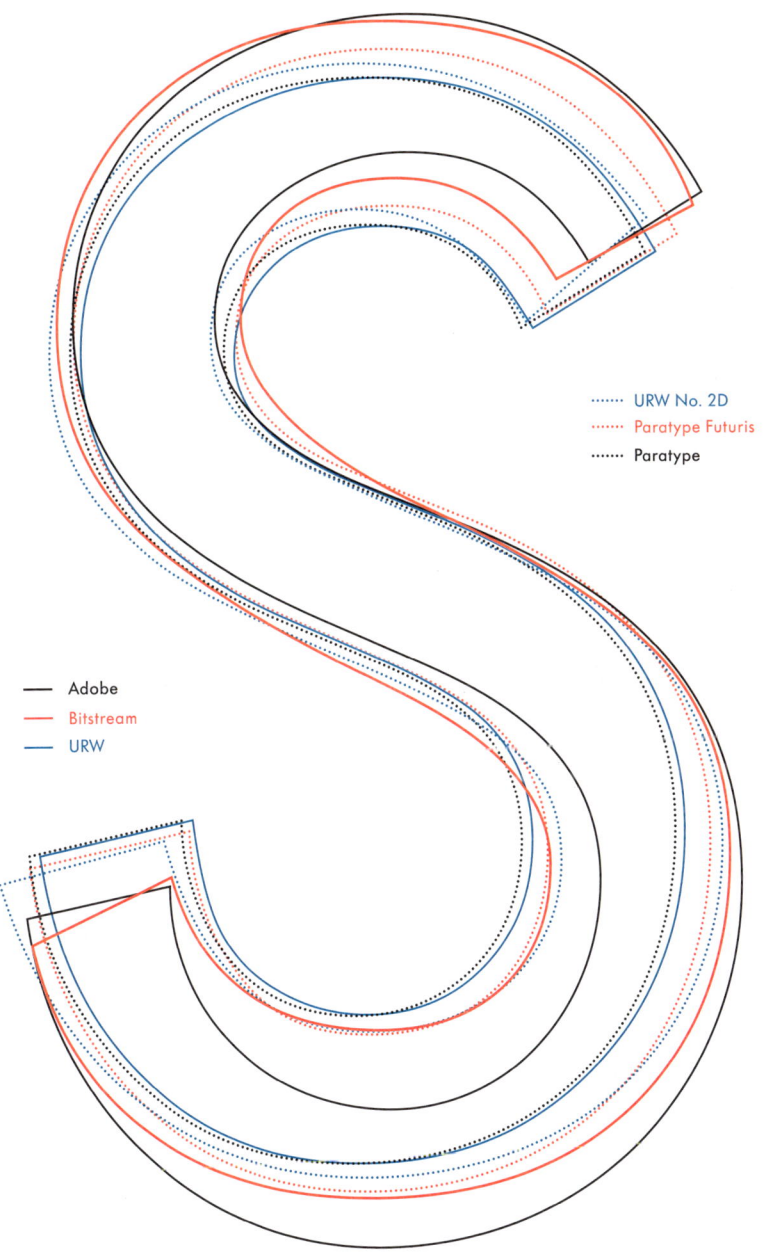

AaBbC
FfGgH
KkLlM
PpQqR
VvWw
Adobe

cDdEe

IiJjKk

NnOo

SsTtUu

xYyZz

Bitstream

Strangers ACN

ELSNER & FLAKE, 1985 Digitized by Veronika Elsner and Günther Flake. Similar to Paratype and URW, the family includes additional heavy weights.

Strangers ACN

TYPESHOP, 2006 Walter Florenz Brendel created gradated weights of existing digital typefaces. Was part of the Elsner & Flake collection until 2006.

Comparison of commerically available digital iterations of Futura in Medium weight at 32 points (right) and at 625 points (opposite)

Strangers ACN

SCANGRAPHIC SB, 2004 Based in part on Elsner & Flake's Futura. Also available in a headline size with tighter spacing and optical adjustments. The Barbican uses Scangraphic for its designs.

Strangers ACN

BERTHOLD, 2000 A new interpretation by Dieter Hofrichter. Is rare in use, in part because Berthold requires licensing the entire type family rather than à la carte purchases.

Strangers ACN

NEUFVILLE DIGITAL, 1999 Digitized fonts from the Barcelona-based offshoot of Bauer by Marie-Thérèse Koreman. Claims to be the most authoritative version, used by Nike.

Strangers ACN

PL FUTE, 2014 Also known as Photo-Lettering Futura or Futura Maxi. Created with large x-heights for exceptionally small sizes by Victor Caruso in 1960; digitized by Photo-Lettering. Monotype released this digital version in 2014.

WE NAMED OUR SHOES AFTER A WOMAN

Nike was the Winged Goddess of Victory in Greek Mythology. Legend tells us she had a mystical presence, and helped to inspire victorious encounters on history's earliest battlefields.

We chose the name Nike because we build shoes that help inspire victory—in athletic contests all over the world.

The shoes of champions.

We put a swooshmark on the side of every pair to symbolize the winged goddess of victory. And also to show people you're wearing the finest athletic shoes available.

Nike. We make all kinds of shoes, for all kinds of women and men and children. And winners.

Try on a pair and fly away from the competition.

8285 S.W. Nimbus Ave. Suite 115
Beaverton, Oregon 97005

6

SHOW ME THE MONEY

ON FRIDAY NIGHTS at an upscale mall in suburban Baltimore, a group of teenage guys gather in the food court to inhale fried meats and soda, hang out, and flirt with other flocks of friends and acquaintances. They are dressed head to toe in their finest consumer brands: Nike, Adidas, and Under Armour, with an astonishing array of semiotic distinctions that would make Saussure's head spin.

At the heart of many of those distinctions, whether on a small tag or proudly emblazoned in large letters, are typefaces—upscale brands in delicate well-spaced serifs or street-smart athletic brands in bold sans serifs. Consumer culture is built directly on small visual cues made even more nuanced. At the heart of most of Nike's advertising and product design is the typeface Futura. Teens wearing Nike at the mall remind me that Nike and Futura have persisted in consumer culture for decades. It's a surprising and persistent phenomenon. Despite everything that Futura has meant, intentionally and unintentionally, it's still cool. Seeing the

PREVIOUS
Futura has been used by Nike from its inception, including this late 1970s advertisement

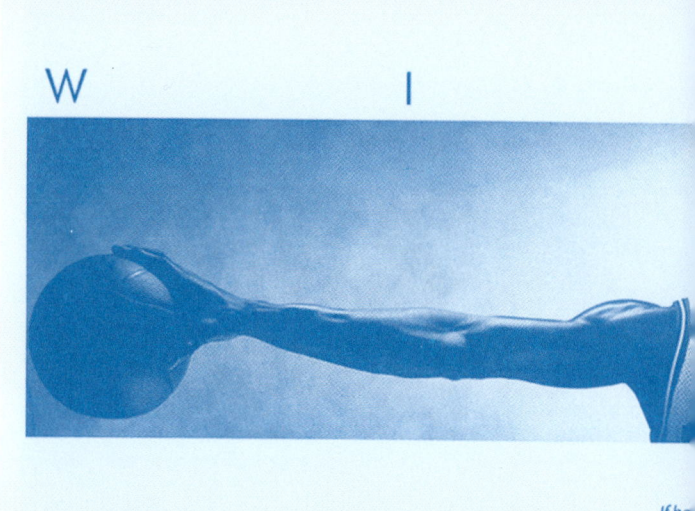

This poster of Michael Jordan, 23 × 72 inches in size, helped make Nike and Jordan iconic.

Futura advertises Nike at every level, including small type on the shoes themselves.

teenagers gawk at and tease each other made my heart pang with my own memories of trying to fit in—and not always having enough money to do so.

From 1988 until 2000 I played basketball on every team I could, starting with city leagues coached by my dad or my friends' dads and progressing up through the high-school varsity team. Every October brought another tryout and a new set of shoes for the new season. Underscoring the constant drumbeat of working harder, hustling more, and trying to win games was the need to look the part. We all wore the same reversible practice jerseys and nylon mesh shorts, so shoes were our only point of individual fashion. Pity to the poor boy who showed up to practice in old shoes or, worse, Adidas, Reebok, or Converse. Technically, our team had no official shoe, but in reality we all wore Nike.

Nike, the once insurgent shoe company, achieved cultural dominance with countless teenage boys in

s too high,
s own wings"
Blake.

the 1980s and '90s by advertising with basketball icon Michael Jordan. His image graced our bedroom posters, our trading cards, and, later, our sneakers. But even in the early days of waffle iron–molded running shoes, and with the first sponsored Air Jordans, Nike spoke in Futura. The Nike logotype sat above the swoosh in slanted Futura Bold Extra Condensed, and the word *AIR*, which announced that special air pocket for flight and comfort was set in Futura Light. And ads pulsed in the hearts of aspiring athletes everywhere with the simple phrase "Just Do It" set in Futura Bold Extra Condensed.

Today Nike and Futura are so fused that almost any phrase in tightly spaced Futura Bold Extra Condensed screams "Just Do It." Look in any sports store and you'll see the T-shirts "Earned Not Given," "Every Damn Day," "Strive For Greatness," and "The Only Way to Finish Is to Start." Many college athletic departments

Nike advertisments have been set in Futura for decades, making Futura Bold Extra Condensed almost as recognizably Nike as its slogan "Just Do It."

JUST DO IT.

SHOW ME THE MONEY

> # FUTURA EXTRA BOLD CONDENSED: THE MOTHER OF ALL TYPEFACES.
>
> It's time for Art Directors the world over to boycott the use of Futura Extra Bold Condensed—the most over-used typeface in advertising history. Destroy the Great Satan of clichés and the Little Satan of naked convenience, and rally to the cause of better type selection.
>
> Please fill out the enclosed petition and mail it to our headquarters. It will be used to sway the opinion-makers of our industry toward our just and worthy cause. Together, we can whip this mother.
>
> **ART DIRECTORS AGAINST FUTURA EXTRA BOLD CONDENSED.**

This ad was designed by Jerry Ketel and published in the Type Directors Club's 1992 *Typography 13* annual.

are completely festooned in the sponsored synergy of Futura, including 68 of the 128 National Collegiate Athletic Association schools in the Football Bowl subdivision.[1] This is no accident. Decades of careful branding work by Nike officials in Beaverton, Oregon, and their advertising partner of record, Wieden+Kennedy, have created this typographic signifier. It's almost like they own it. Of course, when Nike started using it, Futura wasn't the company's or anyone else's—it was already ubiquitous.

Nike chose Futura with good reason: Futura Bold Extra Condensed works well for advertising headlines. It's visually punchy and packs in a lot of words per line.

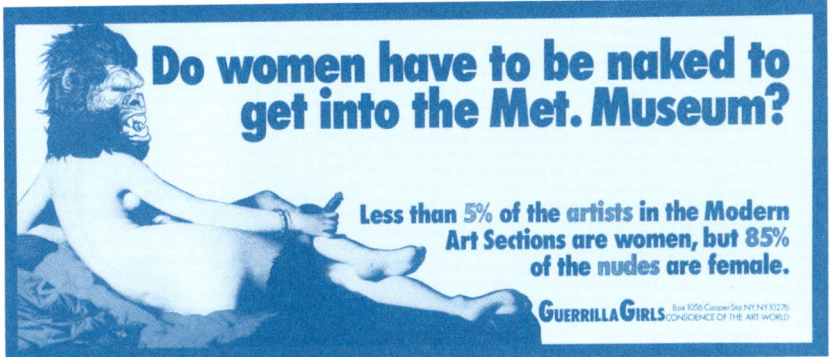

Of course, effective ads always inspire copies. Take a quick look at magazines from the 1980s and you'll see that early Nike ads were typographically similar to those of dozens of other companies that shouted their wares in Futura or other bold condensed headlines. By 1992 insipid use of Futura inspired a campaign against its use: Art Directors Against Futura Bold Extra Condensed. The campaign proclaimed in the Type Directors Club annual: "It's time for Art Directors the world over to boycott the use of Futura Bold Extra Condensed—the most over-used typeface in advertising history. Destroy the Great Satan of clichés and the Little Satan of naked convenience, and rally to the cause of better type selection."[2]

An anti-Futura Bold Extra Condensed campaign might have shamed some advertisers and designers into employing other typefaces, but forward-looking art directors had pushed their work into new territory long before Futura Bold Extra Condensed became a cliché. Others, however, found new life in the style by appropriating and subverting the familiar visual language of advertising for other purposes. In 1989 Guerrilla Girls launched an ad decrying the hypocrisy of an art world

Since 1989 Guerilla Girls have fought sexism with confrontational ads in Futura Bold Extra Condensed.

OVERLEAF In 1987 Sharp Hartwig Advertising used Futura Bold Extra Condensed to advertise dinosaurs at the Pacific Science Center in Seattle.

SHOW ME THE MONEY 135

ACTUAL

DINOSAURS AT PACI

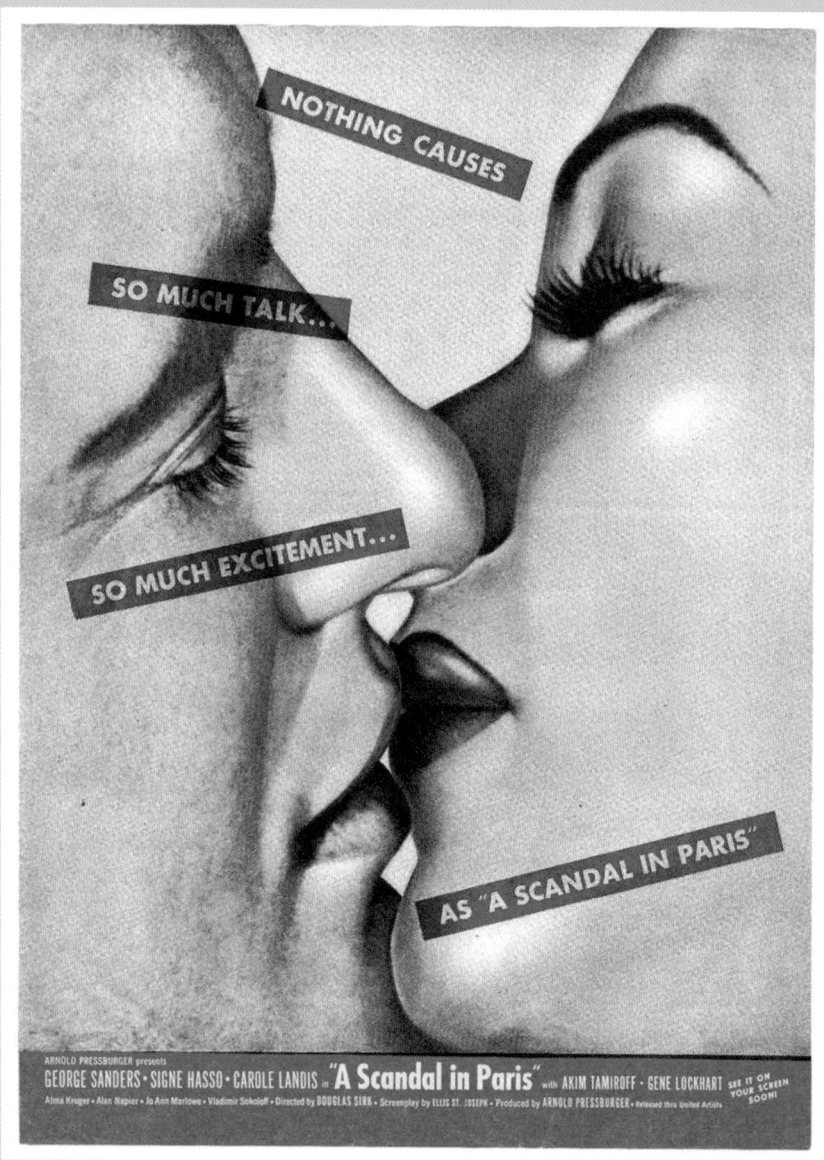

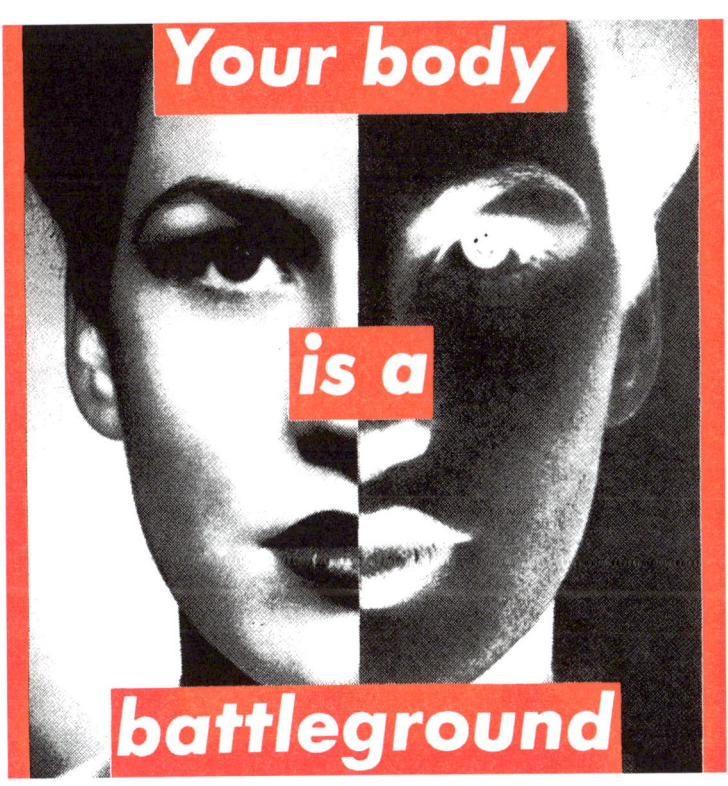

OPPOSITE The 1946 film *A Scandal in Paris* was promoted using a variety of posters. The tight cropping of the kissing stars and bold typography (in Futura) would later inspire Barbara Kruger.

ABOVE Barbara Kruger destabilizes expected designs by creating an appearance of words and pictures cut from advertisments and pasted together. The subverted medium makes the message more poignant.

that valued white male artists over women and minorities. The group's critiques of the entire art establishment resounded (and sadly still do): "Do women have to be naked to get into the Met. Museum?" Or "When Racism & Sexism Are No Longer Fashionable, What Will Your Art Collection Be Worth?"[3]

Antiestablishment critiques are powerful on their own, but they have a deeper bite when wrapped inside the visual language of establishment advertising. At first glance they blend in, but their content is all the more apparent and subversive for borrowing the very means that establishment corporations use in advertising—in this case, a tired visual trope. Would the iconoclasm be as poignant if it were wrapped in visual styles already divorced from the mainstream? By appropriating an advertising style using Futura Bold Extra Condensed, Guerrilla Girls gives its words the same cultural weight as anything produced by any major corporation owned by white men. Typography is legitimacy. Use a different typeface and the message is easier to dismiss.

In 2012 Ellen Hochberg used Barbara Kruger's visual language to criticize conservative policies on women's reproductive health.

The work of Barbara Kruger similarly questions the relationship of consumption and identity by using Futura. Bold, tightly cropped photographs with short declarative words are made to look like advertisements that have been cut and pasted together into critical commentary: "Your body is a battleground," "Money can buy you love," "I shop therefore I am," and "Our prices are insane!" Her work punctures the mythos of a feminine perfection derived from consumer purchase.[4] Her posters and installations, created throughout the 1980s and early '90s, simultaneously appropriate the common visual language of Futura and create an iconic style of her own. For many, Barbara Kruger is Futura Bold Oblique on a red rectangle. And yet, how can

Supreme sells its wares wrapped in visual styles made famous by others. Its logo uses the red box and Futura Bold Oblique that Kruger pioneered.

anyone own a typeface or a style? Easy: put your own ironic anticonsumerist message on a T-shirt or hoodie in Futura, and you can buy and sell your own commodity fetishes.[5]

Build your brand big enough with Futura and you can even sell your egalitarian, anticorporate utopia on the free market. Since 1994 the boutique store started by James Jebbia, called Supreme, in Lower Manhattan, has sold dozens of consumer goods clothed in Futura Bold Oblique in a red rectangle. The company uses a logo that steals Kruger's subversive design, and makes mainstream ad campaigns and dozens of products with Futura emblazoned for all to see, restarting the semiotic cycle of hero worship. Ironically, however, once someone else created a series of shirts labeled in

ABOVE Barbara Kruger's famous crtique of commercial culture, set almost exlusively in Futura Bold Italic.

OPPOSITE Supreme appropriates Barbara Kruger's iconic use of Futura Oblique in a red rectangle to sell a winking critique of commercialism.

Jenny Holzer uses Futura Bold Extra Condensed extensively in her projection art, including this piece at the Guggenheim in New York 2008.

a similar style, Supreme sued for millions of dollars in damages, citing copyright infringement.⁶ In the same vein, Shepard Fairey's Obey Giant campaign started as an anti-advertising street campaign before metastasizing into a clothing brand sold in malls all across the country.⁷ And yes, the original "OBEY" is all Futura Bold Extra Condensed Oblique.

Of course, this has happened with many brands and other typefaces. But in the summer of 2015, as I walked around a mall, dozens of shops still advertised their wares in Futura, including many aimed at women—Forever 21, Louis Vuitton, and, at least for that season, much of the advertising of Banana Republic, J. Crew, and Madewell. Women often get a bad rap for having expensive tastes, being fiercely loyal to their luxury brands, and needing to dress with distinction, but in a way, guys have a more difficult consumer brand hierarchy to climb: with fewer acceptable brands to wear, if you want to fit in, it's all about the money. In fact, a feel-good story made its social media rounds about a young boy who was being bullied at school for wearing the wrong shoes. To help him out, another boy in his school brought him a pair of LeBron James Nike shoes so that he wouldn't be mocked in class, and was given a big hug.[8] In a less brand-saturated age, the moral of the story might have been that brands don't matter; we love you all the same. But in today's harsh world, you need the right brand to measure up.

We are well past the stage of self-parody. All we are waiting for is the government-issued commemorative postage stamps of antiestablishment advertising in Futura, and the circle of appropriation will be complete. Futura represents hero worship, antiestablishment critiques, and everything in between. We think it holds all these meanings, but the real message is that ad agencies and their corporate clients are capitalizing on our earnest desires, from fitting in with the team to raging against the machine. Those desires are spun by the corporate mill of production straight into commerical gold (with special editions for higher-paying customers).

Shepard Fairey built his antiestablishment consumer brand using Futura Bold Extra Condensed Oblique.

FLAT FRONT -BUTTON FLY

DOCKERS® **K-1** KHAKIS

CRAMERTON®
Army Cloth
CUT FROM THE ORIGINAL CLOTH™

SF - California, USA

7

PAST, PRESENT, FUTURA

GROWING UP, Sunday afternoons meant dinner with grandparents, followed by sleepy adult conversation around the table. Often I entertained myself by poking around basements, garages, and storage rooms. There I encountered new worlds in dusty bookshelves and file cabinets filled with old photos, books, and documents. For my parents and grandparents, these keepsakes conjured rich memories, reawakened long-forgotten episodes, and reacquainted them with friends, family, and loved ones. Since I was innocent of life experience, the same artifacts transported me into a past of my own imagination. I re-created scenes as if they were the present, even though my vision was frustrated by musty paper, fading photographs, and narrative holes.

In the late 1990s and early 2000s, three designers revived Futura to evoke collective memories of the mid-twentieth century.[1] Although each of them wielded the past to a different end, their designs helped usher in a flourishing of Futura for their time.

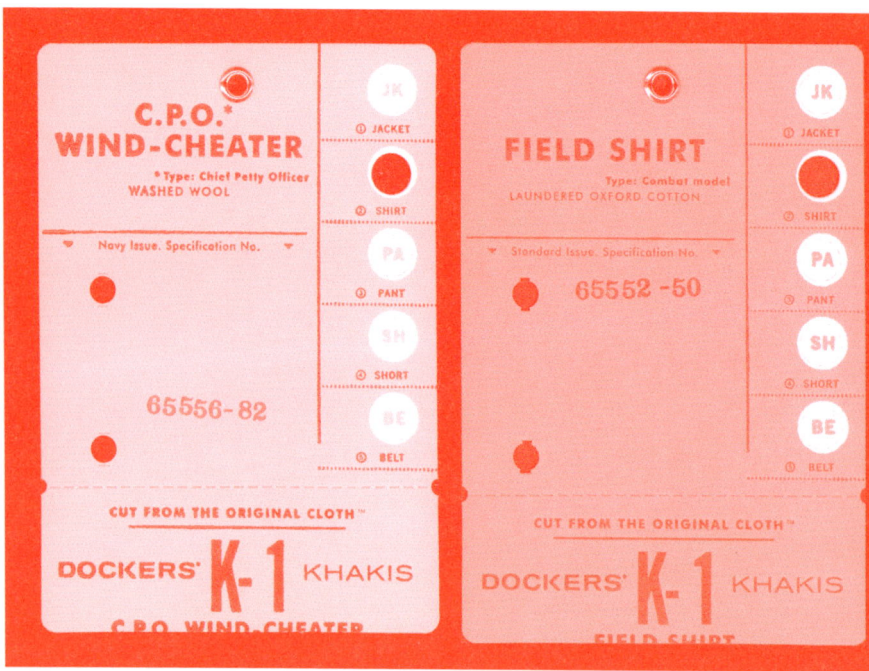

PREVIOUS AND ABOVE Dockers resurrected a World War II–era line of khaki pants in part through careful use of Futura to evoke the past in labeling, packaging, and advertising.

In 1999 work-clothes icon Dockers decided it was time to resurrect its original line of khaki pants. The pants would be completely authentic: they would be made in the same production facilities in Cramerton, North Carolina, feature the same molds for buttons, use the same fabric blends, and follow the same patterns as the 1940s-era khakis made famous during World War II. Dockers approached the San Francisco–based design agency Templin Brink to build a new brand in collaboration with their product designers. For Gaby Brink, design partner at Templin Brink, the solution seemed obvious: create a design system that reflected the same historical accuracy and attention to detail as the new product itself.[2]

For Brink, the impulse to create authentic design had long informed her design process. In the case of Dockers, this meant extensive research into 1940s military packaging and uniforms. The new line of khakis was designed so that it "looks and behaves so authentically, one might well believe the U.S. Army created it in the 1930s."[3] This line of thinking paved the way for every design decision. Labels were created using era-appropriate silk-screen and letterpress printing. The naming scheme for the product line employed a military-sounding letter-number acronym: K-1. As she describes it, "The K-1 brand experience was designed to look decidedly un-designed—fonts, typographic treatments, materials and production techniques are indiscernible from materials produced by the U.S. Army during the 1930s and '40s."

For Brink and Dockers, crafting authenticity meant using Futura in workaday, hot-stamped industrial uses. In this carefully constructed environment, Futura harkens back to World War II and its values. For Brink, "K-1's appeal comes from nostalgia for an era when integrity meant durability and an honest day's work. It was a time of war and economic depression, when women began wearing pants and handling blowtorches. Gritty, gutsy can-do is K-1 ethos."[4]

Dockers's K-1 values are hammered home with thoughtfully curated advertising statements: "Made When Style Was Government-Issue," "Made When the Only Corners Cut Were Cut by Hand," "Made At A Time When the Name on Your Pants Was Your Own," and "Designed to Match Your Scarf, Gloves, and Acetylene Torch." The ads feature beautiful photographs of 1940s-era tools, medals, and dog tags opposite clothing models in sepia-toned photographs.

DECEMBER

SUN	MON	TUE	WED	THU	FRI	SAT
	1	2	3	4	5	6
7	8	9	10	11	12	13
14	15	16	17	18	19	20
21	22	23	24	25	26	27
28	29	30	31			

FILE RECEI

Ja

SUN	MON	TU
Last Quarter 2nd-31st	New Moon 9th	First Quar 16t
4	5 — Co. 300.19 / Sn. 99 10 / Ke. 11 80 / Ko. 9600	6
11	12 — Co 386.33 / Sn. 101.94 / Rich 11.25 / Kor. 9240 / Ke 4080	13
18	19 — Ke 10.20	20
25	26 — Rich 5.25 / Ko 104 10 / Sn. 89 76	27

OPPOSITE Financial planning calendar for small businesses, 1959. Numbers in Linotype Spartan, small type in Kabel (sold as Sans Serif in the United States), Cheltenham, and Century Schoolbook.

BELOW In 2007 Aaron Draplin and Coudal Partners joined to produce Field Notes—a brand built on simple notebooks and calendars for hardworking American industrial workers and nostalgic millennials, all typeset in Futura.

Each ad features the tagline "Cut from the Original Cloth" in Futura Bold, stamped on what looks like an actual clothing tag.

The authentic clothes stamp is a lovely touch that references an era when Futura had achieved widespread popularity. Not only was Futura at the forefront of new typographic trends and designs, it had conquered overlooked side labels and information captions as well. Unlike its earliest avant-garde uses in America and Europe, the Futura referenced by Brink was mass-produced and highly functional: hot stamped in aluminum or offset printed on disposable packages and tags across America.[5]

Dockers' ads, labeling, and precise packaging helped the brand and its parent company target hip young consumers. Cleverly marketed nostalgia allows common, coarse khaki pants once sold cheaply at department stores to be stocked at expensive boutiques and sold for double or triple their ordinary price.[6] Even if Dockers revived a line of cotton pants, the design was not a strict reprinting. The design of both the pants and the packaging, while following cues to align with the past, is done for a new purpose: to attract young audiences steeped in their own vain imagination. Military clothing was never a high-end consumer good.

From the military to the Midwest farm, Futura has meant quality, simplicity, and no-frills dependability. Like Dockers (but without the institutional memory of a long-standing company), Aaron Draplin looks to America's industrial past for design inspiration, product sales, and a taste of authentic American life. His design and self-image embody relics of midwestern cultural values. He loves thick lines and well-crafted

Meyer Seed Company sign, Baltimore. All type seems sexy and fresh when it is new. In part because of weathered signs and faded prints, our perception of typefaces changes as they age.

logos. One of Draplin's design conference talks, entitled "Tall Tales from a Large Man," starts with a mix of religious revival, rock concert, and testimonial. His slides and his shouting celebration of everyday design move with the beat of his music—and the cheers of the crowd. Occasionally, he ends with a self-referential slide: "F**KING FUTURA in 960 POINT TYPE!!!" Bam, bam, bam.

Today there is no greater promoter of Futura than Draplin. Since 2007 his Field Notes series has pushed forward a design aesthetic that references the industrial heartland of American production and a legacy of well-crafted materials long before lumberjacksexuals and Brooklyn hipster brands received widespread attention. Perhaps apropros to his image, Field Notes had humble beginnings. A few years

FIELD NOTES®

FN-01

SET OF THREE
Graph Paper
48-PAGE MEMO BOOKS

3-1/2" × 5-1/2"
Three Staples

FIELD NOTES®
PROUDLY PRINTED AND MANUFACTURED IN THE U.S.A.

Durable Materials
Pocket Size

after leaving a corporate job and going freelance, he designed and hand-printed the first round of memo books as a promotion for his practice. He sent them to friends, designers, and clients throughout the country, and one ended up at Coudal Partners in Chicago. Coudal thought it was worthy of a bigger audience and partnered with Draplin to print and distribute a larger quantity of the notebooks.

Field Notes rebel against the antiestablishment postmodern aesthetic of Draplin's mentors, resurrecting the workman-like designs of industrial America.[7] Draplin's simple design is inspired by thousands of notebooks he's rescued from landfills at estate sales, antique stores, and junk drawers. Most are simple memo books distributed to American farmers and used throughout the American heartland.[8] For Draplin the notebooks represent "regular people working really hard."[9] He celebrates the utilitarian design of each of the memo books, with their careful production and layout—the craft of jobbing printers that typeset and crafted simply. For him they are "really cool and really American."[10]

Draplin's standard Field Notes notebook is small enough to fit into a shirt pocket, filled with lined pages, and bound with thick brown craft paper. The imprint "FIELD NOTES" is printed in Futura Bold on the cover and looks like it was printed decades ago. The simplicity is deceptive, with prudently spaced and meticulously placed type that belies its utilitarian look.

In a way, the notebooks represent Draplin himself. As a midwestern designer who now lives in Portland, Oregon, his motto is "Work hard and do good work for good people." And the design of Field Notes is true to who he is: a notebook for the everyday workman,

OPPOSITE
Field Notes 48-page memo book, typeset exclusively in Futura

not afraid of getting dirty, with no pretense. On why he loves Futura: "It's readable. Holds its own at small sizes, both upper and lower case. I appreciate that versatility.... I just really identify with its utilitarian quality. It works. Might not be the prettiest, but it gets the job done. Like me!"[11]

In 2017 Field Notes have a cult following that, despite itself, is becoming a mainstream audience. Multiple times a year, new editions come out in unique colors and papers—all with the same Futura Bold title on the cover, and in the same size and format as the ones before. They are distributed in limited editions, which quickly sell out from the dedicated Field Notes website and a nationwide network of local shops. A recent edition evidences the collection's acclaim and appeal: Draplin and the CBS News anchor John Dickerson, himself a Field Notes collector, collaborated to create a reporter's-style Field Notes notebook, complete with Wire-O-bound flip-top pages and a modified, but still Futura Bold, title.[12] This addition, like Draplin's vast secondhand notebook collection, speaks to the human romance of scrawled notes, creative doodles, and incomplete thoughts, and celebrates that yesterday's ephemera and commonplace tools are today's prized possessions.

The two-dimensional flatness of Draplin's designs echoes the midcentury authority of hundreds of other sources, including encyclopedias, textbooks, and reference charts. Calling on that same aesthetic, Wes Anderson's *The Royal Tenenbaums* features Futura in a starring role. The first shot of the film is of a novel of the same name set in Futura. The opening titles then mimic the book-cover treatment, pink Futura Bold in front of a green curtain flanked by two

Charles S. Anderson perfected the process of remixing midcentury illustrations and type—including Futura—in his own work and through his eponymous archives. His first book (left) was released in 1995.

candlesticks. The next seven minutes of the prologue walk through each major character's backstory with a cascade of dysfunctional life details. Each story is cataloged by Alec Baldwin's narration and titled in plain, white Futura Bold.

The prologue, set to "Hey Jude," is a journey through the Tenenbaum children's best and worst days growing up and the root of their adult traumas.

OPPOSITE
Wes Anderson creates a fictive past through carefully currated images, sets, wardrobes, and the use of Futura throughout the film *The Royal Tenenbaums*.

The colors, the Beatles, the clothing, and Futura all evoke not only quirky individualism but also a fictive past, labeled as an artifact or museum display. The authority of these labels is cemented by the centered Futura titles appearing throughout the prologue.

In context and style, the use of Futura in film titles and on book covers deliberately conveys shadows of the 1960s. Here, as for Brink and Draplin, typefaces work as an ideal illustration of era—they are referential and just specific enough to place the story in a time frame without crowding the narrative with explicit dates or values. Anderson and his team exploit this purpose well as the film progresses, and titles of the books written by the growing Tenenbaum family change to Milano in the 1970s and Helvetica in the 1980s, marking the passage of time and the aging of characters.

But Futura is a far more active character in the film than just a text on a book cover. The typeface evokes a self-consciously flattened caricature of the past: in the film, Futura appears on the side of buses, museum marquees, posters, ocean liners, and hospitals.[13] Its visual dominance throughout the set heightens the fictive nature of the story, appearing in abundance and to the exclusion of the many other typefaces that would have dotted a real-life scene. Far more than a wider (and technically more accurate) typographic palette would, this effect creates a poignant and nostalgic present that, like all of the characters, is trying to return to an authentic and harmonious relationship between itself and others.

Anderson's use of Futura reflects his own nostalgic past and upbringing as the son of an art director working in advertising and public relations. Anderson

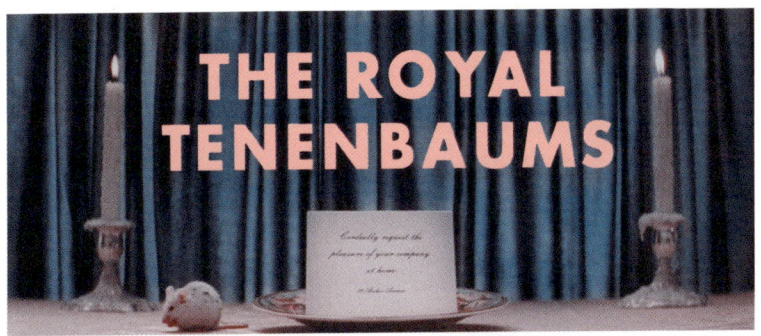

Luke Wilson
as
RICHIE TENENBAUM

The New York City band Vampire Weekend featured Futura Bold on its first three albums *Vampire Weekend* (2008), *Contra* (2010), and *Modern Vampires of the City* (2013).

was raised to understand the meaning of a typeface. In fact, the choice of Futura in his films is not a happy accident of production design, but rather a specific choice by Anderson himself.[14] Futura appeared in the title of his breakout film, *Bottle Rocket* (1998); in *Rushmore* (1999) Futura Bold appeared in a character-sketch sequence similar to the prologue of *The Royal Tenenbaums*. In *Royal Tennenbaums*, even when Anderson's production designers brought him other options, they would always include a Futura option, anticipating that it would be his choice. After several such cycles, his production designers simplified the process and went straight to Futura.[15]

Futura became a trope for Anderson after appearing in several subsequent films. It was even listed on internet guides (*Slate*, the *Huffington Post*, and others) that parody his quirky style as "the Wes Anderson Font."[16] Other guides (some satirical, some serious) champion Futura Bold as the ideal complement to readymade hipster logos, with the formulaic *X* with four identifying icons placed in the cardinal spaces of the grid.[17]

For Brink, Draplin, and Anderson, Futura evokes the past. But also for each, in its use for present projects, Futura is transformed by nostalgia into an exclusive consumer product. For the creators, the reference point to their past remained pure, but like all memories reconstituted in the present, Futura changes in the retelling. It became, and continues to become, a new memory, a new idea, and a new past for others to remember fondly.

Lemon.

e boat.
ove compartment
placed. Chances
ced it; Inspector

r Wolfsburg fac-
ect Volkswagens
3000 Volkswagens
more inspectors

than cars.)
 Every shock absorber is tested (spot c
ing won't do), every windshield is sca
VWs have been rejected for surface scra
barely visible to the eye.
 Final inspection is really something!
inspectors run each car off the line onto
Funktionsprüfstand (car test stand), tote u
check points, gun ahead to the auto

8

FUTURA BY ANY OTHER NAME

"IS VOLKSWAGEN CONTEMPLATING A CHANGE?"
This nearly forgotten headline kicked off the 1959 American Volkswagen Beetle ad campaign—perhaps the most celebrated advertising campaign of the twentieth century.[1] Volkswagen's advertising firm, Doyle Dane Bernbach (DDB), was uniquely tasked with advertising a car that looked essentially the same year after year. The firm's job might have seemed boring, especially because the main competitors were driving sales and recognition with ever-changing looks, colors, and materials. DDB's solution is now canonized in design as much as the car is canonized in midcentury American life: counter the culture, embrace the authentic consistency, and spice it up with witty takes on common sense.

That first VW ad continues: "The answer is yes. The Volkswagen changes continually throughout each year. There have been eighty changes in 1959 alone. But none of these are changes you merely see. We do not believe in planned obsolescence." Unlike the colored fins and shiny chrome spilling off Detroit assembly lines, the Volkswagen Beetle changed where it mattered most—only under the hood.

Like the Beetle's measured unpretentiousness, the VW ad campaign mixed convention with the unexpected, blunt, and self-assured. A typical full-page VW ad started with a two-thirds-page photo atop a headline and three columns of text. This format was known as the old "JWT No. 1," after its longtime use by advertising company J. Walter Thompson. Like the car, the ad began breaking rules on the interior. Terse headlines like "Think Small" and "Lemon" underneath simple photographs dared viewers to consider the car on its own merits. Unlike competitors', VW ads eschewed the normal status markers of midcentury car owners: model families, trimmed lawns, and rambler houses.

True to his modernist outlook, the VW campaign's art director, Helmut Krone, set the headlines and text in Futura. Over time, as the VW Beetle transformed beneath the hood, the ads adopted a reverse scheme, showing signs of following the exterior fashion as photography budgets grew, layouts found new grids, and images became increasingly abstract. All the while, however, the tone of the ads remained consistently, confidently subversive. Visually, DDB quietly kept one choice: the use of Futura. With this, Futura came to epitomize VW's brand identity, if not its immortal reputation.[2]

At the most elemental level, typography—and consistent typeface choices—sells brands and holds together corporate identity. Corporations rely on custom typefaces to distinguish their marks and messages from competitors', while keeping them tethered to the industry's larger image. It is enough to catch a

PREVIOUS, ABOVE, AND OVERLEAF
Volkswagen ads became famous in part through consistent use of Futura.

In 2015 Volkswagen debuted a new custom typeface by MetaDesign, after nearly sixty-five years of using Futura.

glance at the latest tagline on a Nike shirt, because its typographic language will always reference "Just Do It." We readily distinguish the store brands, and even stores themselves, from the name brands of our favorite products, through a happy mixture of color, logo, and typeface.

In 1995, after decades of using Futura, VW faced a problem: it wanted to create billboards with the typeface, but lacked digital versions the company's design team felt would be up to the task. VW commissioned Berlin firm MetaDesign, headed by Erik Spiekermann, who in turn recruited Lucas de Groot, to draw a new digital Futura calibrated for specific sizes. The final products, called VW Headline (for large type) and VW Copy (for small text), came out in 1996, just in time for VW's dramatic relaunch of the Beetle in 1998.[3] Christian Schwartz, then interning with MetaDesign,

NEVER USE FUTURA

Has the Volkswagen fad died out?

Never.

Come in and kick it around.

Impossible.

The 1962½ Volkswagen.

Lemon.

If our bug is too small and our box is too big,
how about something in-between?

Think small.

And if you run out of gas, it's easy to push.

WEATHER

FRONT & CENTER

Caribbean hurricanes were once given the name of the **saint** on whose day they hit. (Like the San Felipe Hurricane on Sept. 13, 1876.)

On this day in **1980**, Phoenix set its October high temperature record of **107 degrees**.

CAN CRICKETS TELL YOU THE TEMPERATURE?

Yes. Count the number of chirps in **14 seconds**, then **add 40**.

TODAY'S

Olympia 72
Salem 76
Port... 76
Bend 68
Eureka 62
Sacramento 77
San Francisco 72
Fresno 79
Los Angeles 86

Alaska

Anchorage

created a lighter weight of VW Headline for the firm's 1999 European ad campaign.[4] Like its predecessor, the new typeface (if not the car itself) became the standard of VW's identity for the next twenty years. In 2015 VW adopted a completely new custom typeface (also by MetaDesign), and ended its continuous use of Futura as the carrier of its global identity.[6]

At the most basic level, new type designs are created to solve printing and technical problems. After 125 years of publication, the *Wall Street Journal* went to Tobias Frere-Jones and Jonathan Hoefler in 2007 to design typefaces that would help cut printing costs. The team created a typeface called Exchange, for the news stories, and another called Retina, for listing stock prices. Their designs allowed the *Journal* to fit the same information in a smaller space while making text and numbers more legible in extreme printing conditions: high-speed offset printing on cheap newsprint, often at exceptionally small type sizes (smaller than 6 point).[7]

In larger sizes, newspapers confront unique challenges: how to fit a large amount of headline text into small spaces, maintain unity across print and digital platforms, and print clearly on cheap, disposable paper. *USA Today* asked foundry Bold Monday to create a custom Futura for its 2014 newspaper redesign. The basic, bold letters in the masthead and the standard bold weight look similar to a normal Futura. However, the condensed headlines are strikingly original, while maintaining a genealogical link to the Futura model. This face is less condensed than normal Futura Condensed. Like many early twenty-first-century typefaces, the *USA Today* typeface raises its x-heights and expands the counters to achieve better legibility at small sizes. Of course, the whole system was developed

Since September 15, 1982, USA Today's masthead has featured Futura Bold.

The 2014 redesign by Wolff Olins imagines a logo that is dynamic as the news: the circle holds new graphics everyday.

OPPOSITE
USA Today's custom-made Futura

USA Today debuted custom versions of Futura called Futura Today in a 2014 redesign, with a unique Bold Condensed for headlines.

simultaneously with web fonts for seamless online experiences on any number of devices. The resulting typeface bears a cousin-like resemblance to the original, but it is by no means a dusty copy of Futura Bold Condensed.

Although Nike uses the Neufville version of Futura Condensed Extra Bold, it commissioned Neufville for a custom version just for the brand, called Nike 365 Condensed Extra Bold. Given Nike's normal usage of Nike 365, any differences the company may have requested are indistinguishable from its original (but not from other digital Futuras). Likewise, most designers can't distinguish Ikea Sans from Futura, the famous typeface that inspired it, or between most corporate typefaces and their commercial precedents. What these corporations buy, besides careful trimming and tailoring, is the same thing that every customer buys with a good suit of clothes: a name and a story. That name, even if it is hidden in the HTML or CSS code, or buried in a corporate style guide, tells every employee (or campaign staffer) that the design has been thought out. Details matter to us. If we use this typeface, we can speak with one voice.

Even while some corporate typefaces are shallow glosses on existing models, most highly original new typefaces began as bespoke faces for corporate clients. Corporations that have the incentive, and capital, can have a typeface that fits their specific needs and uses. For a type designer, it's much easier to design within these defined constraints and contexts than to try making something that will be perfect for everyone, everywhere. Just as in clothing, one-size-fits-all typography may get a job done, but will never look as tailored. The constraints of a technical brief and of corporate needs make a typeface easier to design.

In 1968 the type designer Adrian Frutiger was approached by advertising firm Crosby/Fletcher/Forbes, representing British Petroleum (BP), to consult on a new typeface for the corporation.[8] Frutiger suggested several possible sans serif solutions, including a proposal to revive Herbert Bayer's Universal typeface for BP's uses. Instead, BP requested Futura. In a nod to that request, Frutiger created a customized version of Futura, based on Futura Bold, that was improved for large sizes and given a hint of unique character. In clear contrast to Futura's vertically chopped letter *C*, Alpha BP's letter *C* has terminals at 45-degree angles. These are carried through on several other letters, such as lowercase *g*, *j*, and *r*. In addition, the capitals *B*, *E*, *F*, and *T* are widened. Significantly, the capital *M* is squared, not triangular. The numbers are also more distinct: the number 1 has a diagonal serif; the terminals on 6 and 9

Ikea Sans, a custom version of Futura, was designed by Robin Nicholas for Ikea. Ikea ditched Futura in August 2009 for the web-friendly (and cheaper) default Verdana.

curve around the circle shape. Despite these changes, the similarities between Alpha BP and Futura outweighed the differences, especially in the lowercase. Frutiger himself corroborated that Alpha BP was never made from scratch. "It is an attempt to create a more geometrical Futura," he explained. It undoes many of the subtle optical corrections Renner made for Futura, such as the tapered bowl or curved joints to open the counters, and differences in stroke widths. Renner's optical edits improved Futura's legibility at small sizes, but made the typeface less systematic.[9]

As with most custom typefaces, Alpha BP's distinct name insured that the typeface would be correctly used in every design application, from products to advertisements. In spite of BP's careful attention to this level of detail, however, Futura managed to replace Alpha BP on several product labels and designs—an evidence of Futura's ubiquity and the difficulty of creating a watertight corporate system.[10]

BP's desire for a Futura-like typeface may have been fueled by a conscious (or unconscious) desire to appear friendly to consumers and fit in with the competition. In similar pursuit of the friendly charm of a geometric sans serif (though a few years before BP), the Chermayeff & Geismar studio used Futura as inspiration for a new typeface for Mobil Oil Company.[11]

Custom typefaces officially start with requests in boardrooms and from marketing teams. But many begin quietly in a designer's eccentric interests and personal side projects. Designers are generally pleased to have a client foot the bill that carries their sketches into fully functioning typographic systems. Along these lines, Lucas Sharp's eponymous Sharp

ABCDEFGHIJKLMN
OPQRSTUVWXYZ
abcdefghijklmnop
qrstuvwxyz012345
6789(.,:;-)!?/&

ABOVE Alpha BP Bold, designed by Adrian Frutiger for British Petroleum, 1968

BELOW Herb Lubalin created lettering for *Avant Garde* magazine that became the basis for a typeface designed in 1970–77.

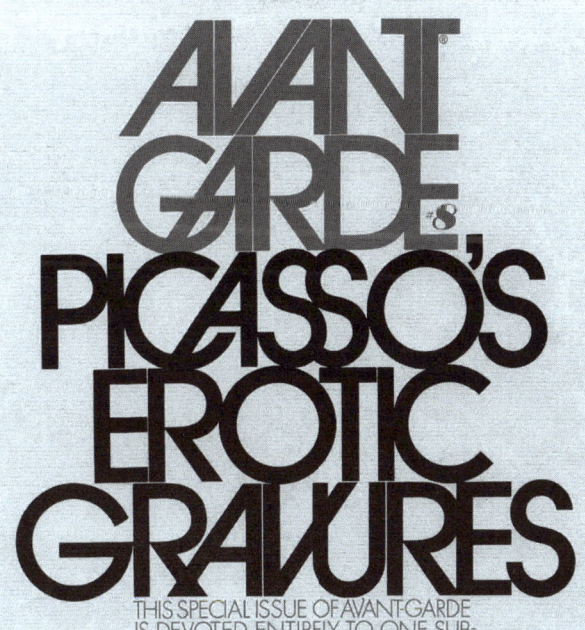

Sans series started as the designer's personal homage to 1970s typography in 2013. Sharp drew specifically on Futura (in its phototypeset iteration), Frutiger's Alpha BP, and Herb Lubalin's Avant Garde, as well as other geometric sans serifs.[12] Sharp expanded on Alpha BP's signature angled terminals, helping make them a defining feature of Sharp Sans and setting it apart from its other typographic forebears. He produced seven weights of the basic text version. And in an unconventional technical turn, Sharp created two distinct display versions, each with ten weights. Display No. 1 embodies Alpha BP in what Sharp describes as a "more humanistic version of Futura" as well as a stylistic set with swash capitals. Display No. 2 re-creates Avant Garde's most distinctive features, such as horizontal terminals and interlocking ligatures.[13]

Soon after Sharp's own version hit the market, he found himself making alterations to suit specific client needs. Among his clients, global electronics behemoth Samsung requested its own custom version of Sharp Sans No. 1. That investment culminated in a new release and name: Samsung Sharp Sans. Another customized version of Sharp Sans No. 1 was prompted by Michael Bierut, a partner at Pentagram, who was considering adopting it for Hillary Clinton's presidential campaign. Pentagram suggested one main change: replacing the square dots over the lowercase *i* and *j* with rounded ones. This seemed minuscule, but would render the typeface "friendlier"—an important feature for a presidential candidate's image.[14] Sharp liked the change well enough to introduce it into the off-the-shelf version of the typeface as well as what became the campaign's custom version.[15]

In addition to the friendly dots, Pentagram and the campaign commissioned other fine-tunings for the typeface. Sharp's modifications automated solutions to basic typesetting problems, creating typographic sophistication that even novice designers and staffers could wield with style and consistency. With the custom Sharp Sans No. 1, known as Unity, as part of a highly constructed system, Pentagram provided the Clinton campaign with a thorough, high-end brand identity that equaled that of any corporate client.[16]

Above all, custom typographic updates help companies feel fresh, while maintaining equity from previous years of success and familiarity. A company might keep the same typeface but make subtle adjustments to its proportion and spacing through periodically revisiting its tailoring—the typographic equivalent to raising a hemline or widening a lapel. The cultural meanings associated with geometric sans serifs generally, or Futura specifically, are carried through the crafted eccentricities of the genre. That's how many new typefaces work: they build off previous greats, while each generation of geometric sans serifs nips and tucks to stay fashionable.

NEVER USE FUTURA?

DESPITE THIS BOOK'S TITLE, you *should* use Futura. When you do, you'll find yourself alongside the pantheon of designers, corporations, and campaigns that made Futura famous. But do so under advisement. To use Futura is to reference a long history of layouts, brands, and platforms. This legendary typeface instantly transmits familiarity and depth of meaning, but it risks just as many unwanted visual associations. Used uncritically, Futura becomes little more than a fetish for the past or a lazy habit. This is one reason that publications, companies, and brands still demand new typefaces. For some, a new typeface that references Futura, yet is clearly unique from it, can reflect Futura's history while introducing fresh and unexpected ideas into the geometric sans serif genre.

Today's typefoundries continue to benefit from demand for fresh takes on old models. Two of this generation's most popular geometric sans serifs come from Hoefler & Co. and House Industries. In 2002 Hoefler & Co. released Tobias Frere-Jones's

PREVIOUS
The typeface Gotham was inspired, in part, by the Port Authority Bus Terminal signage in New York City.

Barack Obama helped popularize Gotham with his victorious 2008 campaign. Poster by Shepard Fairey.

OPPOSITE
The 2010 film *The Social Network* featured Futura both in the film's titles and in its advertising. Neil Kellerhouse's bold typography imprisons Jesse Eisenberg (playing Mark Zuckerberg). Kellerhouse's design separates this poster from typical movie fare and expected uses of Futura.

Gotham for commercial use, after two years as a bespoke typeface for *GQ* magazine. Gotham is a thoroughly American workman's take on the geometric sans serif. It is based on the pragmatic vernacular lettering and engineered metal signage that characterized midcentury US cities, such as the sign on New York City's Port Authority Bus Terminal.[1] Hoefler & Co. expanded the typeface well beyond its initial inspirations by crafting a lowercase, italics, and dozens of weights (from Thin to Extra Black). Gotham quickly rose to popularity, driven in part by its successful use in Barack Obama's victorious 2008 presidential campaign, but also by hundreds of corporate uses worldwide.

Also in 2002, House Industries released Christian Schwartz's Neutraface, a contemporary take on Richard Neutra's 1920s and '30s geometric lettering for Los Angeles building facades. Schwartz describes the Neutraface family as a work of "historical fiction" designed to evoke the era with nods to art deco proportions. His letterforms quote Neutra's uppercase letters, but the lowercase draws upon Neutra's predecessors Futura, Tempo, and Nobel (because Neutra never designed lowercase letters himself). Schwartz conceived of Neutraface as "an ambitious project to design the most typographically complete geometric sans serif family ever."[2] The typeface more than delivers, with dozens of weights and styles that compose the essential toolkit for modern compositions, especially in digital designs with different screen types and sizes.[3]

Of course, after a typeface debuts in society, its cultural meanings cascade from the exclusive to the mass-produced. Amongst trendsetters and fashion-conscious advertisers, Gotham and Neutraface's ubiquity were their demise. A typeface's appearance in

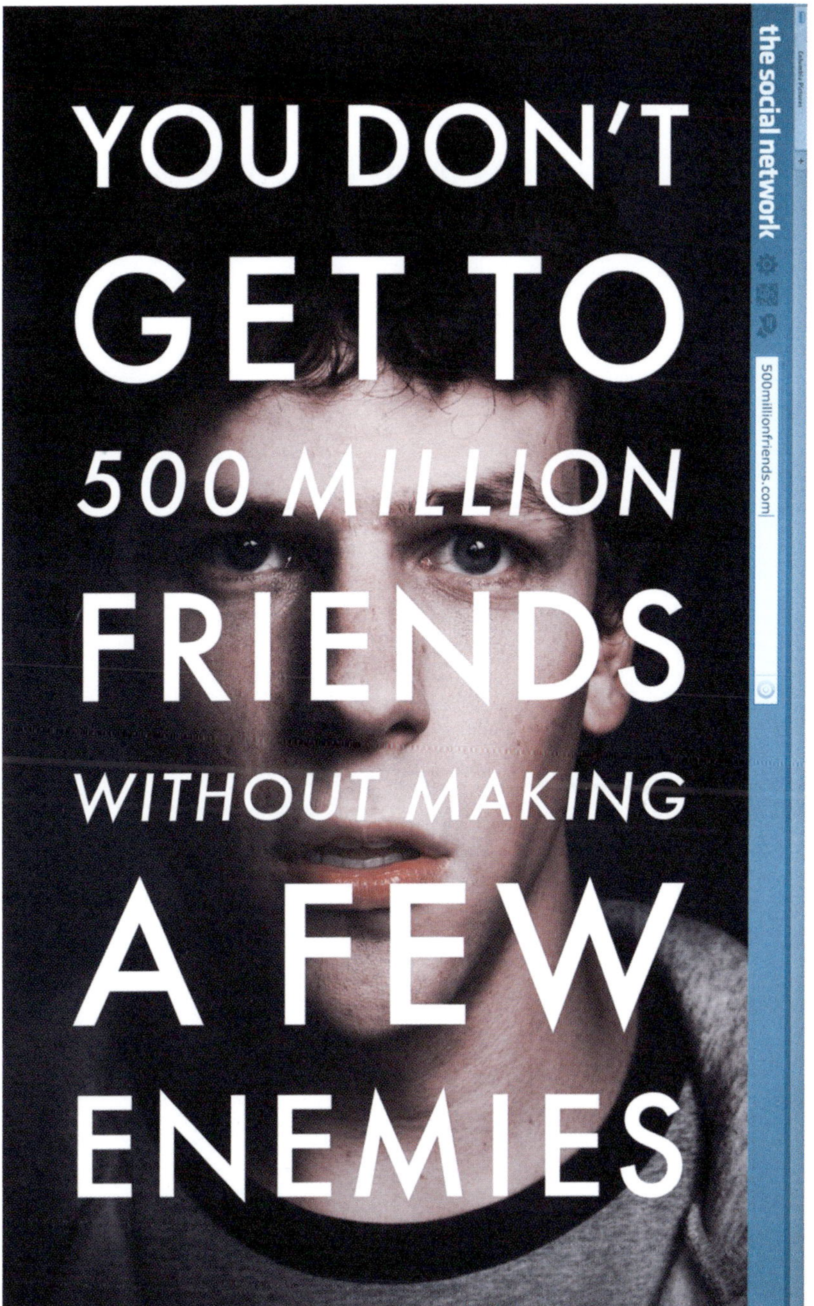

YOU DON'T GET TO 500 MILLION FRIENDS WITHOUT MAKING A FEW ENEMIES

the social network

500millionfriends.com

Some of the most popular contemporary competitors to Futura include two styles of lowercase a, one following the Futura model (in red), the other following the humanistic tradition (in blue).

With each set at 28 points, the apparent difference in size is due to each type designer choosing a different proportion of x-height to cap height.

a Futura

a Avant Garde

a Avenir

a a Proxima Sans

a a Gotham

a a Neutraface

a a Circular

a a Brandon Grotesque

a a Mark

a† a* Eesti

† only available in text weights
* only available in display weights

common use, like convenience-store bathroom signs, local grocery stores, or community colleges, prompts the design industry's elite corps to move on to greener typographic pastures.

Finding and employing the hottest new geometric sans serif is a never-ending quest. Nearly every type designer I know hopes that the geometric sans craze ends and the market won't demand new Futuras. So if you never use Futura, you'll make your local type designer happy (for now). But when geometric sans serifs actually fall from favor, it will be just a few years before it's hot to revive them again.

The search for the perfect geometric sans serif has led working designers and snobbish graduate students to foundries across the world for the next typographic hit. The search might lead you through HVD Fonts's Brandon Grotesque (2009–12), Alias's Ano (2012), FontFont's Mark (2013), Lineto's Circular (2005–13), or Grilli Type's Eesti (2016), just as it led previous generations to ITC's Avant Garde (1970–77), Linotype's Avenir (1988) or Mark Simonson's Proxima Sans (1994).[4]

Even as designers cast about for a new Futura replacement, Renner's ninety-year-old Futura is still a cultural force. The original lead-cast incarnation is rarely seen, used, or even known, but the elegance of the Futura ideal excites the imagination because so many designers have breathed life into the typeface through their own uses, quotations, and adaptations. The key to choosing Futura is to make it your own. Know its history but challenge its past—keep it fresh; make it new. Only in adding innovative voices to the conversation will Futura continue to be the typeface of today and tomorrow. So never use Futura, unless.

ACKNOWLEDGMENTS

DESIGN AND WRITING are team sports. My work has benefited from a lifetime of good coaches and teammates in both camps.

I first came across the advice to never use Futura as an undergraduate at Brigham Young University (BYU). I am perpetually indebted to my first design professors, Linda Reynolds, Adrian Pulfer, Eric Gillett, Ray Elder, Brent Barson, and the late Stephen Hales, for guiding my work, and more importantly, teaching me to find my own answers when I questioned their thinking. BYU's vibrant undergraduate culture also led me to historian Paul Kerry, who encouraged me, as a young designer to study history, and who cultivated a belief that typography is a worthy subject for historical analysis.

The book's subject and framework builds on the work of two design historians: Christopher Burke, whose biography of Paul Renner sparked my academic interest in Futura, and Paul Shaw, whose writings on Helvetica and the New York Subway system inspired the fledgling genre of typographic reception history.

Much of my historical analysis of Futura was born as a master's thesis at the University of Chicago. The intellectual rigor and interdisciplinary climate became the perfect breeding ground for a project like mine. My incipient ideas and research skills received unwavering support and probing from my advisers, Michael Geyer and Sean Dunwoody, as well as in conversations with Jo Guldi, Molly Warnock, Eric Slauter, and Paul Cheney, and my fellow students in Professor Geyer's contemporary history course.

The book's current form took shape at the Maryland Institute College of Art (MICA) under the tutelage of Ellen Lupton and Jennifer Cole Phillips. Their belief in and support of this project propelled my work. Their lessons finessed my ideas and focused my design, and they opened their worlds to me with the faith of true mentors. Elizabeth Evitts Dickenson and David Barringer showed me the storytelling potential of design writing and gave expert feedback on my writing and process. Bob Cicero and Alison Fisher at the Globe Press at MICA introduced me to Futura's first American imposter and the beauty of letterpress. Brockett Horne and Jason Gottlieb gave advice and encouragement at important moments.

My fellow MFA cohort at MICA listened to and saw my ramblings perhaps more than they wished. Special thanks to my fellow type nerds Shiva Nallapernal, Iris Sprague, and Alex Jacque for talking about Futura's intricacies and details, and to Sally Maier and Amanda Buck for conversations about the socioeconomic and political dimensions of typography and design. At a crucial juncture, Henry Becker organized a group of readers for drafts of each chapter. The group helped me connect with readers, and lit a fire under me to keep me writing. Many thanks to the members of that group, Brooke Thyng, Andrew Keiper, Ninad Kale, and Jarrett Fuller.

Thank you to the many people who commented on aspects of this book, with interviews, conversations, or written thoughts: Michael Bierut, Chester Jenkins, Lucas Sharp, Christian Schwartz, Greg Gazdowicz, Tal Leming, David Wasco, Carl Sprague, Joan Winters, Wolfgang Hartman, Paul Gehl, Benedikt Reichenbach, Rianne Petter, Mark Mulder, Gaby Brink, Abbott Miller, Jeremy Hoffman, Amy Redmond, Paul Shaw, and Christopher Burke. Each of them provided insights and helpful corrections.

Librarians and archivists defend our history from the ravages of time. I have been helped by many at the Library of Congress, National Archives, Museum of Modern Art, Cooper Hewitt Smithsonian Design Library, Newberry Library, the Bodleian Library, the Bancroft Library of the University of California at Berkeley, the Harold B. Lee Library at BYU, the Milton S. Eisenhower Library at Johns Hopkins University, the Joseph Regenstein Library at the University of Chicago, and the Decker Library at MICA.

I am grateful to my editor Barbara Darko and her careful readings of the text, and the team at Princeton Architectural Press for their professionalism and attention to detail. Thanks to Susan Clements for her work on the index.

A special thanks to my parents and brother who have listened to dinner-table editions of this book for decades, who in addition to love and support, provided every needful thing to launch a design career, from my first Futura-labeled Crayola crayons to my first iMac.

The idea for making this book began with an unexpected discovery on a library shelf; it grew through dozens of conversations with a friend, then girlfriend, then wife. She has talked repeatedly through every idea, and read through every word—not to mention waiting patiently while I took yet another picture of Futura in the wild. This book never would have happened without her. Thank you, Ruth.

Although this book has had a first-rate team, any errors (factual, grammatical, or typographical) are mine alone.

NOTES

INTRODUCTION: BACK TO THE FUTURA

1. The defaults included on the standard-issue Macintosh include over one hundred type families, most of which include multiple fonts ("Mac OS X v10.6: Fonts list," Apple Support, accessed September 21, 2016, https://support.apple.com/en-us/HT202408). Windows machines have a similar number of default families installed, with even more if you have Microsoft Office installed. Standard-issue design programs, like Adobe Creative Cloud (or its predecessor, the Adobe Creative Suite), add many more families. The current version includes a subscription to the Adobe Typekit library of 2,450+ fonts (accessed September 21, 2016, https://typekit.com/plans). As a student, I also had access to many more, including a library of Bitstream typefaces that included 247 type families, not to mention the possibility of purchasing any number of hundreds of thousands of choices from commercial retailers, or searching out countless others available for free (or pirated) online. The supply of typefaces is not limited; judgment about which ones to use, on the other hand, is.

2. On Futura's place in design histories, see Philip B. Meggs and Rob Carter, *Typographic Specimens: The Great Typefaces* (New York: John Wiley & Sons, 1993), which includes Futura as one of thirty-eight of the "finest type families in the world." Rob Carter, Philip B. Meggs, Ben Day, Sandra Maxa, and Mark Sanders, *Typographic Design: Form and Communication*, 6th ed. (New York: Wiley, 2015) includes Futura as their prime example of a geometric sans serif typeface. Stephen Coles, *The Anatomy of Type* (New York: Harper Design, 2012) notes the place of the typeface in contemporary design: "Futura has become widely known as the prototypical Geometric typeface." Stephen J. Eskilson, *Graphic Design: A New History* (New Haven, CT: Yale University Press, 2012), 232, describes Futura as the "sans serif with the longest-lasting impact on modern typography."

ONE: MY OTHER MODERNISM IS IN FUTURA

1. Alfred H. Barr, *Cubism and Abstract Art* (New York: Museum of Modern Art, 1936), exhibition catalog; most of the chart is typeset in Intertype Vogue, an early competitor to Futura. In fact, to make Vogue look more like Futura, Intertype manufactured alternate characters to match. The distinguishing feature on this printing is the high-waisted crossbar on the capital *A*s and a capital *C* with a much smaller aperture than Futura's flat cropped endings. In 1934 Intertype licensed and adapted Futura for its typesetting machines; see Christopher Burke, *Paul Renner: The Art of Typography* (New York: Princeton Architectural Press, 1998), 111. See also Sybil Gordon Kantor, *Alfred H. Barr, Jr. and the Intellectual Origins of the Museum of Modern Art* (Cambridge, MA: MIT Press, 2003), 314–28; Kantor's book is typeset entirely in Futura.
2. The Bauer Type Foundry, *The Type of Today and Tomorrow: Futura [Type Specimen for the New York Office]* (Frankfurt: Bauer, ca. 1928).
3. For a deeper explication on the evolution of Futura, see Burke, *Paul Renner*, 86–119. See also Alexandre Dumas de Rauly and Michel Wlassikoff, *Futura: Une Gloire Typographique* (Paris: Norma, 2011), 17–36; and Petra Eisele, Annette Ludwig, and Isabel Naegele, eds., *Futura. Die Schrift* (Frankfurt: Herman Schmidt, 2016).
4. Burke, *Paul Renner*, 102n.
5. The Bauer Type Foundry, *The Type of Today and Tomorrow: Futura [Type Specimen for the New York Office]* (Frankfurt: Bauer, ca. 1938–39).
6. Burke, *Paul Renner*, 95–96.
7. For the full chronology of Paul Renner's typography, see Philipp Luidl, *Paul Renner: Eine Jahresage* (Munich: Typographische Gesellschaft, 1978).
8. The *New York Times* gave notice about new typefaces as "jazz types" in 1927 (see "German Printing Praised at Exhibit," *New York Times*, September 7, 1927). Some printers distinguished between jazz typography and other styles (see H. W. Smith, "The Printers Publicity," *Inland Printer*, August 1920). Smith quotes an editorial from Nebraska: "There are two distinct styles of typography: one, the loud, black, erratic display—jazz. The other, the pleasing, simplified style—harmony. The jazz style is intended to excite you to action and is adaptable to the circus, ballahoo, and fire sale variety of business. The harmony style is intended to harmonize your thoughts into well rounded out decision, and is adaptable to anything possessing stability. The former style is much the easier to compose, as it matters little what type you hit upon; the more discord the better." On the racial quality of jazz as an epithet, see Jane Anna Gordon and Lewis Gordon, *A Companion to African-American Studies* (Oxford: Blackwell, 2006), 210–11.
9. "Steile Futura," Fonts In Use, https://fontsinuse.com/typefaces/28702/steile-futura.

10. Ralf Herrman, "The Multifaceted Design of the Lowercase Sharp S (ß)," Typography.Guru, March 16, 2016, https://typography.guru/journal/german-sharp-s-design/ and Ralf Herrman, "Kurrent—500 years of German handwriting," Typography.Guru, February 21, 2015, https://typography.guru/journal/kurrent%E2%80%94500-years-of-german-handwriting-r38/; and Hans Peter Willberg, "Fraktur and Nationalism," *Blackletter: Type and National Identity*, ed. Peter Bain and Paul Shaw (New York: Princeton Architectural Press, 1998). On Futura's place in the German script debate, see Burke, *Paul Renner,* 79–86.

11. Tschichold's first manifesto on the subject, "Die Neue Typographie" (1925), appeared in *Kulturschau*, a literary journal for left-oriented literature, followed by a book under the same name in 1928. See Jan Tschichold, *"The New Typography (Die Neue Typographie),"* in *Active Literature: Jan Tschichold and New Typography*, trans. Christopher Burke (London: Hyphen Press, 2007), 29.

12. Tschichold, "The New Typography," 29.

13. Anthony Julius, *T. S. Eliot, Anti-Semitism, and Literary Form* (Cambridge: Cambridge University Press, 1995), 194.

14. Stephen J. Eskilson, *Graphic Design: A New History* (New Haven, CT: Yale University Press, 2007), 259–60.

15. William Ashe, "Cost and Method: Vanity Fair and Its Modernity Are Killed By Time," *Inland Printer*, April 1930, 85–115.

16. Ibid, 85. For a more equanimous approach to capitalization, see Douglas McMurtrie, "The Cult of the Lower Case," *Modern Typography and Layout* (Chicago: Eyncourt, 1929), recently reproduced in Steven Heller and Philip B. Meggs, ed. *Texts on Type: Critical Writings on Typography* (New York: Allsworth, 2001), 141–45. After describing the emerging trend and contextualizing historically, McMurtrie's concludes that "capital letters are necessary to our reading comfort only because we are used to them. If they are kept to their traditional duties as openers of sentences and announcers of names, perhaps they help a little…we of the present generation would miss them and be a little disconcerted in our reading if they were suddenly everywhere abolished. A later generation, however, brought up on nothing but lowercase letters, would be much more disconcerted if the capitals were as suddenly to reappear" (145).

17. "Proletarian Punctuators," *New York Times*, March 19, 1930.

18. Ashe, "Cost and Method," 115.

19. Ibid.

20. J. L. Frazier and Milton F. Baldwin, "You Didn't Go Wrong on Modernism if You Followed the *Inland Printer*!," *Inland Printer*, April 1930, 77.

21. Ibid.

22. Ibid.
23. "Typographic Scoreboard: *Vogue*"; "Typographic Scoreboard: *Saturday Evening Post*," *Inland Printer*, June 1930.
24. "Typographic Scoreboard: *Vogue*," *Inland Printer*, January 1933.
25. J. L. Frazier, "Typographic Scoreboard: *Vogue*," *Inland Printer*, November 1945, 41.
26. For *Harper's Bazaar*, see Bauer Type Foundry, "Futura: A Modern Bauer Type," *Inland Printer*, July 1930, 18, and for *New Yorker*, see Bauer Type Foundry, "Futura: A Modern Bauer Type," *Inland Printer*, August 1930, 41. Bauer must have had success with the *Harper's Bazaar* numbers, because it ran with them in additional ads in the October 1930 issue of the *Inland Printer* as well.
27. On the use of Futura by American Modernists, see Philip B. Meggs and Alston Purvis, *Megg's Graphic Design History*, 5th ed. (New York: Wiley, 20), 333–65. See also Steven Heller, *Paul Rand* (New York: Phaidon, 2000). In 1953 Alexander Nesbitt gave a talk to the Type Directors Club where he described Futura as "the most used advertising display letter" and that the "early Futura publicity slogan which, translated, said, 'A type conquers the world.' This was more prophetic perhaps than they meant it to be." Alexander Nesbitt, "Futura," in Heller and Meggs, ed. *Texts on Type: Critical Writings on Typography* (New York: Allsworth, 2001), 82–87.
28. Some printers and publishers attempted a boycott of Bauer Futura (and other German typefaces) in 1939. The proliferation of American copies, however, ensured that even if the boycott was successful, the aesthetic of Futura would remain in full force. See chapter 2.

TWO: SPARTAN GEOMETRY

1. For a treatment of many of Futura's competing geometric sans serif, see Ferdinand Ulrich, "Types of their Time—A short history of the geometric sans," *Font Shop*, April 2, 2014, https://www.fontshop.com/content/short-intro-to-geometric-sans.
2. Frederick Taylor, *The Downfall of Money: Germany's Hyperinflation and the Destruction of the Middle Class* (New York: Bloomsbury Press, 2013); and Liaquat Ahamed, *Lords of Finance: The Bankers Who Broke the World* (Penguin: New York, 2009), 215.
3. Loans were secured through J.P. Morgan and the other major financial houses of London, Paris, and Brussels; behind the scenes, US secretary of state Charles Evan Hughes helped shepherd the deal. See Adam Tooze, *The Deluge: The Great War, America, and the Remaking of the Global Order, 1916-1931* (New York: Viking, 2014), 458–61.
4. "Proclamation to Craftsmen, Artisans and Friends of the Graphic Arts" issued by the Graphic Arts Forum in 1939; the boycott was

reported in various newspapers. For example, "Anti-Nazi Boycott in Printing Asked," *New York Times*, July 13, 1939, 9. The *Times* reported the boycott against Nazi types but without reference to specific typefaces. Coincidentally, the notice was flanked by ads on either side typeset in Futura (or Spartan, since it had been recently made available for Linotype—the primary typesetting machine used by the *Times*).

5. Wolfgang Hartmann, letter to author, July 3, 2016. Bauer Type Foundry's original contract with Paul Renner included royalties to 2.5 percent of sales in Germany and 1 percent sold internationally. See contract between Bauersche Giesserei and Paul Renner, July 18, 1927. In 1979 Hermann Zapf provided expert testimony to a German court that established copyright protection for Futura. See German Court Landgericht Frankfurt am Main, November 28, 1979, 2/6 0 418/78. The decendents of Paul Renner continue to receive royalties from all licensed digital incarnations of Futura of 1.25 percent of sales in Germany and 0.5 percent of sales internationally. See License Agreement between Inheritors of Paul Renner with Fundición Tipográfia Neufville, SA, November 5, 1990.

THREE: DEGENERATE TYPOGRAPHY

1. John Heartfield (born Helmut Herzfeld) anglicized his name in protest of German nationalistic jingoism at the beginning of World War I. He opposed the rise of Nazism forcefully in his art and politics. See Andrés Mario Zervigón, *John Heartfield and the Agitated Image: Photography, Persuasion, and the Rise of Avant-garde Photomontage* (Chicago: University of Chicago Press, 2012), 72.

2. On shutting down the Bauhaus by edict, see Magdalena Droste and Bauhaus-Archiv, *Bauhaus 1919-1933* (Berlin: Taschen, 2006), 228-36. For some, time in the United States whitewashed prior collaboration with the Third Reich. On the nature of exiled Bauhaus faculty and students, see Jeannine Fiedler, ed., *Bauhaus*, English ed. (Potsdam, Germany: H.F. Ullmann, 2006), 588-90. On the continuity of Bauhaus ideas and students the in the Third Reich, see Michael Siebenbrodt and Lutz Schoebe, *Bauhaus: 1919-1933 Weimar-Dessau-Berlin* (New York: Parkstone Press), 238.

3. Christopher Burke, *Paul Renner: The Art of Typography* (London: Hyphen Press, 1998), 126-36; and Paul Renner, *Kulturbolshewismus?* (Frankfurt: Stroemfeld Verlag, 2003 [1932]).

4. Kurt Schwitters, *Typographie und Werbegestaltung* (Hannover: n.d. [1930]). Quoted in Burke, *Paul Renner*, 109n.

5. Stven Heller, *Iron Fists: Branding the 20th-century Totalitarian State* (New York: Phaidon, 2008), 49-55. The Nazi party itself was not monolithically against modern typefaces, and in fact adriotly exploited them even as it largely promoted new blackletter type-

faces. For example, see the modernist covers of *Die Jungenschaft* a magazine directed at the Hitler Youth. See Steven Heller, "Don't be Fooled That Sans Serif Type Means Freedom,"*Print*, June 15, 2016, http://www.printmag.com/daily-heller/dont-be-fooled-die-jungenschaft/.

6. David A. Fahrenthold, "Mitt Romney reframes himself as a 'severely conservative' governor," *Washington Post*, February 16, 2012.

7. Yves Peters, "Trajan at the Movies," in *The Eternal Letter: Two Millennia of the Classical Roman Capital*, Codex Studies in Letterforms (Cambridge, MA: MIT Press, 2015).

8. Village,"Sharp Sans," accessed May 3, 2015, https://villg.com/incubator/sharp-sans; Michael Bierut, interview by the author, March 2016; Chester Jenkins, interview by the author, March 2016; Lucas Sharp, interview by the author, April 2016. See chapter 8 for more detail about the creation of Sharp Sans and Unity.

9. On Donald Trump's business branding, see John Cantwell, "Trump the Logo," Design Observer, http://designobserver.com/feature/trump-the-logo/8477; the line in his Trump University Branding 101 course "You do not need a graphic design house to develop your logo" was quoted in Steven Heller, "You Know What Else Sucks About Donald Trump? His Branding," *Wired*, July 7, 2015, https://www.wired.com/2015/08/donald-trump-branding-as-arrogant-as-he-is/; on the general branding of the Trump campaign, see Matt Toder, "2016 Campaign Logos: Trump Goes Modern," NBC News, December 7, 2015, http://www.nbcnews.com/news/us-news/2016-campaign-logos-trump-goes-modern-n475776.

FOUR: OVER THE MOON FOR FUTURA

1. A visit to Cape Canaveral makes this fusion of fiction and reality even clearer to see, even in modern terms: not only is each exhibit accompanied by the soundtracks of space movies quietly playing through ambient speakers, but you can see much of the correspondence between NASA and Disney, whose artists were contracted to design space stations, rockets, and space suits as early as the 1940s.

2. Adam Mann, "The Best Space Images Ever Were by Apollo Astronauts with Hassleblad Cameras," *Wired*, July 20, 2013, http://www.wired.com/2013/07/apollo-hasselblad.

3. Manuals printed for NASA by the McDonell Aircraft company show the first uses of Futura for the space program. See NASA, *Project Mercury Familiarization Manual Manned Satellite Capsule* (St. Louis, MO: McDonell Aircraft Corporation, 1959); NASA, *Project Gemini Familiarization Manual: Rendezvous and Docking Configurations* (St. Louis, MO: McDonell Aircraft Corporation, 1966), including the first successful moon landing. See NASA, *Apollo 11 Flight Plan* (Houston: NASA, 1969). Not all NASA centers used the same printing style

guide. Publications from the Marshall Flight Center in Alabama show less consistent use of Futura. See NASA, *Saturn V Flight Manual* (Huntsville, AL: NASA, 1969).

4. The IRS slowly added Helvetica to its forms throughout the 1980s. Helvetica was used for the large date on the header of the 1040 form in 1983 alongside the sturdy Franklin Gothic. By 1990 it was used for the entire form. The Federal Food and Drug Administration (FDA) codified its guidelines for nutrition labels in 1990, mandating that the head label be in Helvetica Black or Franklin Gothic and all other information in Helvetica. See https://www.irs.gov/pub/irs-prior /f1040--1980.pdf, https://www.irs.gov/pub/irs-prior/f1040--1983 .pdf, https://www.irs.gov/pub/irs-prior/f1040--1986.pdf, and https://www.irs.gov/pub/irs-prior/f1040--1987.pdf, https://www .irs.gov/pub/irs-prior/f1040--1990.pdf. The FDA still mandates Helvetica for the label. See Food and Drug Administration, *A Food Labeling Guide* (College Park, MD: Food and Drug Administration, 2013).

5. The current identity standards for NASA still mandate Helvetica as the primary typeface for communications, even though the logo has since reverted to the original 1959 mark. See National Aeronautics and Space Administration, *NASAstyle*, November 2006.

6. Code of Federal Regulations Section 14, Chapter V, Part 1221, US Government Printing Office, 2011.

FIVE: FUTURA IN THE WILD

1. Christian Schwartz, "Five Years of Commercial Type" (lecture, AIGA Baltimore Design Week, Maryland Institute College of Art, Baltimore, MD, October 22, 2016).

2. Stephen Coles, "Massimo Vignelli's A Few Basic Typefaces," *Fonts In Use*, August 13, 2016, https://fontsinuse.com/uses/14164/massimo -vignelli-s-a-few-basic-typefaces. In 1991 his aphorism was that he only needed a "few basic typefaces." There is no list of twelve, but the number comes from Massimo Vignelli, *The Vignelli Canon* (New York: Vignelli, 2010), in which he wrote: "Personally, I can get along well with a half a dozen, to which I can add another half a dozen, but probably no more." In the book, he begins his list with four: Bodoni, Garamond, Century Expanded, and Helvetica, to which he would add Futura, Times New Roman, Univers, Optima, Caslon, and Baskerville. The other two are unspecified "and a few other modern cuts."

3. John Boardley, "The Vignelli Twelve," *I Love Typography*, April 17, 2010, http://ilovetypography.com/2010/04/17/the-vignelli-12-or -we-use-too-many-fonts/.

SIX: SHOW ME THE MONEY

1. Zach Barnett, "Nike, Adidas or Under Armour: Who Wears What in FBS?," *Football Scoop*, April 2, 2015, http://footballscoop.com/news/nike-adidas-or-ua-who-wears-what-in-fbs.
2. Type Directors Club, *Typography 13: The Annual of the Type Director's Club* (New York: Watson-Guptill, 1992), 91–92.
3. Guerrilla Girls, "Some of our Greatest Hits, Posters, Stickers, Billboards, Books," accessed November 23, 2015, http://www.guerrillagirls.com/posters/index.shtml.
4. Barbara Kruger, *Barbara Kruger: Thinking of You* (Los Angeles: Museum of Contemporary Art, 1999). Barbara Kruger continues to comment on contemporary culture and society, including on magazine covers such as the October 13, 2016 preelection issue of *New York* magazine branding Donald Trump as a "loser" in no small part for his comments against women. Others have been criticized, such as the 2010 *W* magazine cover featuring a nude Kim Kardashian made safe for magazine stands by the careful placement of Kruger's headlines. For an example of the criticism, see Kyle Munzenrieder, "*W*'s 'The Art Issue Starring Kim Kardashian' Sums Up Everything That's Wrong With Art," *Miami New Times*, October 12, 2010.
5. On the irony and effectiveness of copying Kruger, see Michael Bierut, "Designing Under the Influence" in *Seventy-Nine Short Essays on Design* (New York: Princeton Architectural Press, 2012), 170–72.
6. Foster Kamer, "Barbara Kruger Responds to Supreme's Lawsuit: 'A Ridiculous Clusterf**k of Totally Uncool Jokers,'" *Complex*, http://www.complex.com/style/2013/05/barbara-kruger-responds-to-supremes-lawsuit-a-ridiculous-clusterfk-of-totally-uncool-jokers.
7. For the description of the beginnings of the Obey Giant phenomenon, see Shepard Fairey, *Covert to Overt* (New York: Rizzoli, 2015), 14–16. On Fairey's branding as culture itself, see Sarah Banet-Weiser and Marita Sturken, "The Politics of Commerce," in *Blowing Up the Brand*, ed. Melissa Aronczyk and Devon Powers (New York: Peter Lang, 2010), 281.
8. Riley Jones, "Young Sneakerhead Gave a Pair of LeBrons to a Classmate Who Was Being Bullied Over His Shoes," *Complex*, November 17, 2015, http://www.complex.com/sneakers/2015/11/kid-gives-classmate-lebron-sneakers-after-bullying.

SEVEN: PAST, PRESENT, FUTURA

1. On the paradoxes of nostalgia in design, see Jessica Helfand, *The Invention of Desire* (New Haven, CT: Yale University Press, 2016), 140.
2. Gaby Brink, in discussion with the author, April 11, 2016.

3. "Dockers K-1 Khakis," Tomorrow Partners, accessed June 30, 2016, http://www.tomorrowpartners.com/casestudy/dockers-khakis. (Brink was working with Joel Templin for their firm Templin Brink at the time of the project. Her current design firm is called Tomorrow Partners.)
4. Ibid.
5. It is likely that most of the original packaging that Brink referenced in her design work was not printed using Futura but rather Spartan—an American knockoff that closely follows the Futura model. See chapter 2 for more information about Futura and its copies.
6. Stuart Elliott, "The Media Business: Advertising; Levis Strauss adds dashes of youth and sensuality to Dockers," *New York Times*, March 11, 1999, http://www.nytimes.com/1999/03/11/business/media-business-advertising-levi-strauss-adds-dashes-youth-sensuality-dockers.html.
7. Aaron Draplin, *Pretty Much Everything* (New York: Abrams, 2016), 99–103. "About Field Notes: Everything You Need to Know," Field Notes Brand, accessed July 5, 2016, https://fieldnotesbrand.com/contact/.
8. "We Know Where We're From," Field Notes Brand, accessed July 5, 2016, https://fieldnotesbrand.com/from-seed/.
9. Field Notes, "From Seed," video, 8:46, https://fieldnotesbrand.com/from-seed.
10. Ibid.
11. Michael Dooley, "Aaron Draplin on Portland, Pizza, and…Design," *Print*, April 14, 2011, http://www.printmag.com/design-inspiration/aaron-draplin-on-portland-palin-pizza-and-design/.
12. See "FNC-31: Summer 2016—The 'Byline' Edition," Field Notes Brand, accessed July 5, 2016, https://fieldnotesbrand.com/products/byline.
13. Mark Simonson has cataloged the extensive use of Futura in the film on his blog. See Mark Simonson, "Royal Tenenbaum's World of Futura," *Notebook* (blog), August 17, 2004, http://www.marksimonson.com/notebook/view/RoyalTenenbaumsWorldofFutura.
14. Carl Sprague (artistic director for *The Royal Tenenbaums*), interview by the author, July 2016.
15. David Wasco (production designer for *The Royal Tenenbaums*), interview by the author, July 2016.
16. See, for example, *Slate*'s "Wes Anderson Bingo card," http://www.slate.com/blogs/browbeat/2012/05/24/wes_anderson_bingo_play_along_with_moonrise_kingdom_using_our_bingo_board_generator_.html; or *Huffington Post*'s "Fifteen Absolutely Necessary Ingredients for Making a Wes Anderson Film," http://www.huffingtonpost.com/2013/11/06/wes-anderson-movie_n_4225333.html.
17. See, for example, Tim Delger's "The Hipster Logo Design Guide," http://hipsterlogo.com/.

EIGHT: FUTURA BY ANY OTHER NAME

1. Bob Garfield, "Ad Age Advertising Century: The Top 100 Campaigns," *Advertising Age*, March 29, 1999, http://adage.com/article/special-report-the-advertising-century/ad-age-advertising-century-top-100-campaigns/140918/.
2. Despite the fact that Futura is a German typeface, Volkswagen did not impose the choice on Doyle Dane Bernbach. Other advertising firms created ads for other vehicles in VW's lineup, using other typefaces, such as Franklin Gothic.
3. Lucas de Groot, "The Volkswagen Headline and Volkswagen Copy," FontFabrik, accessed December 2016, http://www.fontfabrik.com/fofawor4.html.
4. Christian Schwartz, "VW Headline & Heckscrift," *Orange Italic*, accessed October 2016, http://www.orangeitalic.com/vw.shtml.
5. Alexandre Dumas de Rauly and Michel Wlassikoff, *Un Gloire Typographique* (Paris: Editions Norma, 2011), 168–69.
6. As part of the launch of the new typeface, Xavier Chardon, head of marketing for Volkswagen, said, "A consistent brand experience across all touchpoints around the world is our number-one means of solidifying the Volkswagen brand even more." See Volkswagen case study, MetaDesign, accessed October 2016, http://sanfransisco.metadesign.com/case-studies/volkswagen. See also Jens Meiners, "Das Typeface: Volkswagen Reveals of All Things, a New Font," *Car and Driver*, May 26, 2015, http://blog.caranddriver.com/das-typeface-volkswagen-reveals-of-all-things-a-new-font/.
7. Virginia Postrel, "Playing to Type," *Atlantic*, January/February 2008.
8. In 1972 the same firm would later add two new partners in its global expansion, and recast themselves as Pentagram.
9. Hein Osterer and Philipp Stamm, *Adrian Frutiger Typefaces: The Complete Works* (London: Birkhauser, 2009), 214–16.
10. See ibid., 427n. Today many oil companies draw upon Futura, simultaneously creating and taking advantage of its familiarity and friendliness, to reflect on their industry. Indeed, from its beginnings Futura Bold was pushed for just these uses. One Bauer advertisement from 1929 stated, "Type as powerful, as clean cut, as distinguished as trains themselves, has hitherto been rather a problem. With Futura Bold, conveying the same energetic, abstract and logical qualities, this problem fades to the vanishing point. Never was there a typeface better suited to the present message of not only the railroads but also the entire heavy industries, than this" ("Bauer Type Foundry," *Inland Printer*, June 1929). Oil companies like Standard Oil even printed their motorist maps and area guides in Futura. The Aluminum Company for America's first logo with the acronym ALCOA was designed in Futura. The penchant for oil companies to

use Futura as a basis for its typefaces has stuck: the Dutch Shell Oil uses Futura, and a drive through your local small town in the United States will inevitably greet you with Valero, Liberty, and American Fuel—and there is Maxol in Ireland and Motul in France—all of which appear in versions of Futura.

11. While some corporations seek a Futura with modifications to solve their technical problems, others use Futura as a starting point, looking for a new style. Herb Lubalin famously created a custom typeface for *Avant Garde* magazine, which he also art directed. In contrast to Futura, Avant Garde reintroduces ornamentation and a surprising degree of playfulness. Avant Garde is most well known for its extreme number of ligatures (ways to connect and compress letter pairs). In this, Lubalin maximized the potential of phototypesetting to connect and overlap letters in ways unimaginable in lead type. For a discussion of Lucas Sharp inspirations, see John Brownlee, "The Surprising 1960s Origins of Hillary's Official Typeface," *Fast Company Design*, September 9, 2016, https://www.fastcodesign.com/3063556/the-surprising-1960s-origins-of-hillarys-official-typeface. Brownlee states in his interview: "In addition to picking up influences from ITC Avant Garde, [Sharp] was also inspired by Futura, Avenir, Gotham, and 'Frutiger Frutiger Frutiger.'"

12. Village,"Sharp Sans," accessed May 3, 2015, https://villg.com/incubator/sharp-sans (site discontinued). The May 2015 iteration of the website introduced the typeface in terms of Futura: "Lucas Sharp's first release through Village debuts in the Incubator. Sharp Sans injects some much needed humanism into the Futura model. With its sheered terminals and true italics, Sharp Sans combines the appealing typographic compensation of the grotesque, with the plump circular bowls of the geometric. The result is a typeface suited for both text and display use that breaths life into the genre of the geometric sans." The current site describes Sharp Sans in terms of the typeface Avant Garde. Village, "Sharp Sans," acessed February 20, 2017, https://vllg.com/sharp-type/sharp-sans.

13. Michael Bierut, interview by the author, March 2016; and Chester Jenkins, interview by the author, March 2016.

14. Lucas Sharp, interview by the author, April 2016.

15. Perhaps unsurprisingly, given both the designer's and client's attention to detail, the campaign capitalized even on the typeface's name to drive their message home to staffers, designers, and, subconsciously, voters. At their request, the Hillary Clinton campaign's custom typeface is named Unity.

EPILOGUE: NEVER USE FUTURA?

1. "Gotham History," Hoefler & Co., http://www.typography.com/fonts/gotham/history/.

2. Christian Schwartz, "Neutraface," Schwartzco, http://www.christianschwartz.com/neutra.shtml; Neutraface was art directed by Ken Barber and Andy Cruz, and released in 2002 by House Industries (see https://houseind.com/hi/neutraface).

3. In fact, Schwartz's discontent with the appearance of Neutraface in small text sizes, and the appearance of ersatz alternatives to the typeface by graphic designers, led him to revisit the typeface. Neutraface No. 2 raises the crossbars and optimizes the letterforms for longer bodies of text. See "Neutraface No. 2," Schwartzco, http://www.christianschwartz.com/neutra2.shtml; and Alissa Walker, "How The *New Yorker* Redesigned For the First Time in 13 Years," *Gizmodo*, September 17, 2013, http://gizmodo.com/how-the-new-yorker-redesigned-for-the-first-time-in-13-1325328771.

4. Brandon Grotesque (2009–10) and Brandon Text (2012) are designed by Hannes von Döhren and published by his type company, HVD Fonts. Döhren also helped design FontFont's FF Mark (2013) with Christoph Koeberlin and the FontFont Type Department. Laurenz Brunner designed Circular (2005–2013) for Lineto. Alias's Gareth Hague designed Ano for *Another Man* magazine (2006), before releasing it to a wider audience in 2012. GT Eesti (2016) is a revival of the 1947 Soviet typeface Zhurnalnaya Roublennaya by Anatoly Schukin, designed by Reto Moser, Tobias Rechsteiner, and the Grilli Type team. ITC Avant Garde (1970–1977) began as a logo for *Avant Garde* magazine designed by Herb Lubalin, 1968. It was developed into a typeface in partnership with Tom Carnase and released by International Typeface Corporation (ITC) in 1970. Condensed weights were added by Ed Benguiat in 1974, and obliques by André Gürtler, Erich Gschwind, and Christian Mengelt in 1977. *Avenir* is the French word for future. Adrian Frutiger considered Avenir (1988) his paramount achievement. It was released by Linotype in 1988. It was expanded into a larger family with Akira Kobayashi between 2004 and 2007 and given the name Avenir Next. Proxima Sans was begun in 1981 as sketches by Mark Simonson, but first released as a commercial font in 1994 through FontHaus. It was reworked beginning in 2003, and released in 2005 under the name Proxima Nova. With Proxima Nova's availabilty on Typekit in 2009, it became one of the most popular interface typefaces on the planet.

IMAGE CREDITS

27 Alfred Barr, "Cubism and Abstract Art," Digital Image © The Museum of Modern Art/Licensed by SCALA / Art Resource, NY.

36-37 Pablo Picasso illustrations to "love, and the genleman with the monocle," *Vanity Fair*, October 1929. © 2016 Estate of Pablo Picasso / Artists Rights Society (ARS), New York.

42 Image of Alvin Lustig cover design of *The Great Gatsby*, New Classics, New Directions, 1945. Courtesy of Ned Drew.

46 Futura letterpress image from Daily Type Specimen.

48 Bauer Futura / American Type Founders Spartan comparision image courtesy Amy Redmond, Amada Press, Seattle. The type is originally from the collection of Stern & Faye, Printers, and was carefully curated by C. Christopher Stern.

57 Boycott on Nazi Types, MSS 2000/84CZ Box 1 Folder 1, courtesy of The Bancroft Library, University of California, Berkeley.

60 Futura Medium, Acme Wood Type and Manufacturing Co., *Catalog No. 20*, 1937, and Moderna Bold, American Wood Type Manufacturing Co., *Catalog No. 36*, 1936. Images courtesy of David Wolske.

64 John Heartfield, "Neider Mit Den Kreigshetzern!" Kämpft für die Sowjetunion!," © 2016 The Heartfield Community of Heirs / Artists Rights Society (ARS), New York / VG Bild-Kunst, Bonn.

66 "Hilter! The faith and hope of millions" handbill, courtesy of University of Minnesota Library.

69 John Heartfield, "Das letzte Stück Brot raubt ihnen der Kapitalismus," © 2016 The Heartfield Community of Heirs / Artists Rights Society (ARS), New York / VG Bild-Kunst, Bonn.

72 John Heartfield,"Der Sinn Hitlergruss," *A-J-Z*, © 2016 The Heartfield Community of Heirs / Artists Rights Society (ARS), New York / VG Bild-Kunst, Bonn.

86 Apollo 11 Moon landing plaque, National Aeronautics and Space Administration (NASA), 1969.

88 *2001: A Space Odyssey* film poster, Metro-Goldwyn-Mayer, 1968.

88 Apollo 11 mission patch, National Aeronautics and Space Administration (NASA), 1969.

89 Mercury-Atlas 6 orbit chart, United States Air Force, 1961.

90–91 Hasselblad used in Apollo 11 mission, National Aeronautics and Space Administration (NASA), 1969.

92 O_2 sensor controls, Apollo 11 mission, National Aeronautics and Space Administration (NASA), 1969.

93 Daily meal packets, Apollo 11 mission, National Aeronautics and Space Administration (NASA), 1969.

136–37 Dinosaurs at Pacific Science Center advertisement, courtesy of Sharp Hartwig, Inc.

139 Barbara Kruger, "Your body is a battleground," courtesy of the artist.

140 Ellen Hochberg, "Who does she think she is?," 2012.

142 Barbara Kruger, "I Shop, therefore I am, " courtesy of the artist.

143 Supreme street photograph, © Stefan Georgi, 2012.

144 Installation view from Jenny Holzer: For the Guggenheim, Solomon R. Guggenheim Museum, New York, September 26–December 31, 2008.

159 Film stills, Wes Anderson, dir., *The Royal Tennenbaums.*

179 *The Social Network* film poster, © 2010 Columbia Pictures Industries, Inc., and Beverly Blvd LLC. All Rights Reserved. Courtesy of Columbia Pictures.

INDEX

Page references for illustrations appear in *italics*.

1936 Olympics, 68
2001: A Space Odyssey (Kubrick), 87, 88, *88*

Aaron's, 114
Acme Wood Type & Manufacturing Co., 61
Adidas, 131, 132
Adler, 67
Adlerwerke, 67
Adobe Creative Suite, 107
Adobe Futura, 63, 107, 124, 125, 126-27
advertising and branding, 88-89, 92, 94, 98-99, 101, 130-45, 146-61, 162-75
Agha, Mehemed, *36-37*, *38*, *39*, 52
Airport Gothic, *51*, *52*, *55*, *59*
Akzidenz-Grotesk, 14, *84*
Akzidenz-Grotesk Bold Extended, *84*
Albers, Josef, *35*
Aldrin, Buzz, 94
Alias, 181
Alliance '90 (Germany), 76, *76*
Alpha BP, 171-72, *173*, *174*
Alternative für Deutschland (Germany), 76, 76-77
American Printer and Lithographer, 21
American Type Founders, 50, *51*, *56*
American Wood Type, *61*
Anderson, Charles S., 157
Anderson, Wes, 156-58, *159*, 161
  Bottle Rocket, 161
  The Royal Tenenbaums, 156-58, *159*, 161
  Rushmore, 161

Ano, 181
Apollo missions. *See* NASA
Apple Store Genius Bar, 110
Arbeiter-Illustrierte-Zeitung (Workers Pictorial Newspaper), 72
Arial, 59, *84*
Armstrong, Neil, 94
art deco, 26
Art Directors Against Futura Bold Extra Condensed, 135
Avant Garde (magazine), 173
avant-garde (style), 95, 99, 152
Avant Garde (typeface), *80*, *84*, *173*, *174*, *180*
Avenir, *180*, 181

Baldwin, Alec, 157
Baltimore Type Foundry, *51*, *52*, *55*
Banana Republic, 144
Barcelona, Spain, 68
Barr, Alfred H., 25, 27
Bauer Futura, 32, *33*, *48*, *49*, *51*, *56*, *59*
Bauer Topic, *33*
Bauer Type Foundry, 25, *26*, 28-29, *29*, 45, 46, 47-48, 48-49, *51*, *52*, *53*, *62*, *63*
Bauhaus, 22, 25, *26*, *35*, 67
Bayer, Herbert, *35*, *35*, *43*, *45*, *99*, 171
Baynesville Electronics, Towson, Maryland, 117
Beatles, 158
Beaverton, Oregon, 134
Bed Bath & Beyond, 112
Belgium, 72
Berlin (typeface), 165
Berlin Wall, 76

INDEX 201

Berthold, 48, *49*
Berthold Futura, 63, *128*, *129*
Berthold-Grotesk, 48, *49*
Best Buy, 112
Beware of Dog, *120*
Bible, 33
Bierut, Michael, 174
big-box stores, *112–15*
Big Kmart, *113*
Big Lots, *113*
Bitstream Futura, 62, *124*, *125*, *126–27*
blackletter, *34*, 35, 66, *66*, *67*, 68, 72, 73
Bodoni, 21
Bold Monday, 169
Bolton Hill, Baltimore, Maryland, *12*
Bottle Rocket (Anderson), 161
Boycott Nazi Type!, *57*
Boy Scout Handbook, *79*
BP. *See* British Petroleum (BP)
Brand New (blog), 21
Brandon Grotesque, *180*, 181
Brendel, Walter Florenz, 129
Brigham Young University, 15
Brink, Gaby, *148–49*, 152, 161
British Monotype, *54*, 56
British Petroleum (BP), *171–72*, *173*
Bündus 90/DieGrünen. *See* Alliance '90 (Germany); Green Party (Germany)
Bush, Jeb, 81, *84*
Butti, Alessandro, *58*

Cameron, David, 74
Cardi, Alma Reese, *99*
Caruso, Victor, *129*
Caution: Automatic Door, *121*
Caution sign (on maintenance vehicle), *121*
CBS News, 156
Century Schoolbook, *150*
Cheltenham, *150*
Chermayeff & Geismar, 172
Chicago, Illinois, 15, 21, 53, 155
Christie, Chris, 81
Circular, *180*, 181
Civil Defense, *95*
Civilian Exclusion Order No. 1, *78*
Claire's, *108*

Clinton, Hillary, 81, *81*, *82*, *84–85*, *174–75*
Collins Food Market, *116*
Comic Sans, 14, 19
Communication Arts, 21
Communist Party of Germany, *64*, 69
Communists, *64*, 66
Conservative Party (UK), 74, *74*, 76, *77*
constructivism, 22, 25
Container Corporation of America, *43*
Continental Type Founders Association, 48
Converse, 132
Costco Wholesale, *112*
Coudal Partners, *151*, 155
Cramerton, North Carolina, 148
Crayola crayons, *18*
Crosby/Fletcher/Forbes, 171
CSS (code), 171
Cuba, *102*
cubism, 25, 27
Czechoslovakia, 72

Dadaism, 25
Damon, Matt, 101
Dangerous Drop, *120*
Danne & Blackburn, *98*, *99*
Dawes Plan, 48
Dawson, Richard, *79*
DDB. *See* Doyle Dane Bernbach (DDB)
DD's Discounts, *114*
Deberny & Peignot, 56
Degenerate Art. *See* Entartete Kunst
Design Observer, 21
Dickerson, John, 156
Die Kunst der Typographie, *33*
Die Linke (Germany), 76, *76*
digital typefaces, 30, 47, 59, 62, *62–63*, *124– 25*, *126–27*, *128–29*, 163, 169, 170
Dix, Otto, 68
Dockers, *146*, *148*, *148–49*, 152
Dolce & Gabbana, *109*
Doyle Dane Bernbach (DDB), 163, 164
Draplin, Aaron, *151*, *152–53*, *155–56*, *158*, 161
"Tall Tales from a Large Man," 153
Dwiggins, W. A., 53

Eesti, 181
Eisenhower, Dwight D., 73, 74, 75
electric pole, Harrington Park, New Jersey, 104
Elegant-Grotesk, 48, 49
Eliot, T. S., 35, 38
Elsner & Flake Futura, 63, 128
Entartete Kunst, 67-68, 73
Erbar, 26, 49, 49
Erbar-Grotesk, 48
EuroGiant, 115
Europe (typeface), 56
Exchange, 169
Exploring Mars (Gallant), 97
Exploring the Moon (Gallant), 99

Fairey, Shepard, 144, 145, 178
Federal Building, 118
Field Notes, 151, 153, 154, 155-56
Fincher, David
  The Social Network, 179
Findlay, Bruce and Esther
  Your Rugged Constitution, 79
Fire Department, Baltimore, Maryland, 118
Fire Exit sign, 120
FontFont, 181
Forever 21, 108, 144
Fraktur, 33, 34, 35
France, 33, 48, 56, 72
Franklin Gothic, 73, 76
Frazier, J. L., 40-41, 44
Frere-Jones, Tobias, 77, 169, 177-78
Frutiger, Adrian, 171, 172, 173, 174
Fundación Tipográfica de Richard Gans, 58
Futura Black, 30, 31, 73
Futura Bold, 30, 31, 64, 73, 108, 112, 113, 114, 115, 118, 119, 120, 121, 122, 123, 152, 156, 161, 161, 169, 171
Futura Bold Condensed, 30, 31, 116, 170
Futura Bold Condensed Oblique, 76
Futura Bold Extra Condensed, 133, 134, 134, 135, 136-37, 140, 144
Futura Bold Extra Condensed Oblique, 144, 145
Futura Bold Italic, 142
Futura Bold Oblique, 30, 112, 114, 140, 141, 141
Futura Book, 30, 31
Futura Book Oblique, 30
Futura Condensed, 108, 169
Futura Condensed Bold, 120
Futura Condensed Extra Bold, 170
Futura Custom, 117, 118
Futura Display, 30
Futura Extra Bold, 113, 114, 122, 123
Futura Extra Bold Condensed, 116
Futura Inline, 30, 31
Futura Kräftig, 30
Futura Light, 108, 109, 110, 111, 112, 113, 114, 117, 118, 133
Futura Light Condensed, 30
Futura Light Oblique, 30, 31
Futura Maxi, 128, 129
Futura Medium, 109, 110, 111, 114, 117, 120, 124
Futura Medium Oblique, 30, 31, 121
Futura Oblique, 143
Futura Schmuck, 29
Futura Semibold, 30, 31
Futura Semibold Condensed, 30
Futura Semibold Oblique, 30
Futura Today, 170. See also USA Today
Futuria, 59
futurism, 25

Gallant, Roy
  Exploring Mars, 97
  Exploring the Moon, 99
Garamond, 74
Garamond, Claude, 26
Garamond Bold, 81
Geno's Steaks, Philadelphia, Pennsylvania, 116
German National Election, 66
Germany, 33-35, 34, 35, 45, 47-48, 49, 56, 57, 58, 66-69, 72-73, 76-77
Gill, Eric, 54, 56
Gill Sans, 54, 56, 59, 76, 87
GitHub, 63
Glenn, John, 89, 94
Goldwater, Barry, 75
Golf Galaxy, 115

INDEX 203

Google Docs, 59, 64
Google Fonts, 63
Gotenburg, 67
Gotham, 74, 77, 176, 177-78, 178, 180
Gotham Slab, 77, 77
Goudy, 19
GQ, 22, 178
Granby, 58
Graphis, 21
Green Party (Germany), 76, 76
Grilli Type, 181
Groot, Lucas de, 165
Grotesca Radio, 58
Guerrilla Girls, 135, 135, 140
Guggenheim Museum, New York City, 144
Gutenberg, Johannes, 33

Hamilton Manufacturing Company, 60
Harper's Bazaar, 45
Hasselblad 500EL, 89, 90-91
Heartfield, John, 66, 72
Helvetica, 14, 22, 80, 98-99, 99, 101, 101, 158
Helvetica Neue, 59
Hess, Saul, 51
Hitler, Adolf, 66-69, 67, 69, 85
Hochberg, Ellen, 140
Hoefler, Jonathan, 77, 169
Hoefler & Co., 177-78
Hoefler & Frere-Jones, 77, 77, 81
Hofrichter, Dieter, 129
Holzer, Jenny, 144
House Industries, 177, 178
HTML (code), 171
Huffington Post, 161
Humphrey, Hubert, 75
HVD Fonts, 181

Ikea, 171
Ikea Sans, 170, 171
Inland Printer, 21, 22, 40-41, 44, 45
International Typeface Corporation (ITC), 19, 80
Intertype, 51, 52, 52-53, 79
ISOTYPE, 95
ITC. *See* International Typeface Corporation (ITC)

jackboot letters, 66-67. *See also* blackletter
James, LeBron, 145
Jannon, Jean, 26
Japanese internment, 78
Jazzways, 24
J. Crew, 144
Jebbia, James, 141
Jews, 38, 70-71, 72, 73
Johnson, Lyndon B., 75
Johnston, Edward, 56
Jordan, Michael, 132-33, 133
Joyce, James, 38
JWT No. 1, (J. Walter Thompson), 164

Kabel, 26, 48, 49, 49, 53, 59, 66, 119, 150
Kandinsky, Wassily, 68
Kellerhouse, Neil, 179
Kennedy, John F., 75
Kennedy, Robert F., 75
Ketel, Jerry, 134
KIPP, Washington DC, 117
Klee, Paul, 68
Klimschs Jahrbuch, 35
Klingspor, 48, 49, 49
Koreman, Marie-Thérèse, 129, 208
Kristall Grotesk, 48
Krone, Helmut, 164
Kruger, Barbara, 139, 140-41, 142
Kubrick, Stanley, 87
  2001: A Space Odyssey, 87, 88, 88
Kurrentscript, 33

Lanston Monotype, 51, 53
Latin Script, 33
Lenin, Vladimir, 39
Letraset, 124
Liberty (USA), 123
Limited (store), 109
linecasting, 50, 53
Lineto, 181
Linotype, 50, 51, 52, 53, 53, 56, 62, 150, 181
Linotype Futura, 63
Los Angeles, California, 178
Louis Vuitton, 109, 144
Lubalin, Herb, 173, 174
Ludlow, 51, 53, 53, 56, 59

Ludwig & Mayer, 48, 49, *49*
Lukoil, *123*
Lupton, Ellen,
   Thinking with Type, 14
Lustig, Alvin, 42, 45
Luther, Martin, 33

Madewell, 144
Make America Great Again, *83*
Make Up Forever, Dublin, Ireland, *111*
Marathon (USA), *122*
Mark (typeface), *180*, *181*
Martian, The (Scott), 101
Maryland Institute College of Art (MICA), 15, 20
Maxol (Ireland), *122*
Mercury (typeface), 81
Mercury missions. *See* NASA
Meta, 84
MetaDesign, 165, *165*, 169
Metro, 52, 53, *53*, 56
Meyer Seed Company, *153*
MICA. *See* Maryland Institute College of Art (MICA)
Microsoft, 84, 85
midcentury, 15, 75, 96, 99, 156, 163-64, 178
Middleton, Robert Hunter, 51, 53
Milano, 158
Mobil Oil Company, 172
Mode, 61
Moderna, 61
modernism, 36-37, 38-41, 44-45, 73, 76, 94-95, 101
Moholy-Nagy, László, 45
monolinear, 29
Monotype Futura, 63
Monson, Cal (campaign), *80*
Morris, William, 22
M Salon, Federal Hill, Baltimore, Maryland, *111*
Museum of Modern Art
   Cubism and Abstract Art, 25, 27

NASA, *86*, *88*, 88-89, *89*, *90-91*, *92*, *93*, 94, *98*, 98-99, *99*, *100*, 101, *101*
   Apollo missions, *88*, 88-89, *92*, *93*, 94, 101
   Mercury missions, 95

National Collegiate Athletic Association, 134
nationalism, 33-35, 38
National Socialists (Germany), 66
Nation's Business, 44
Nazis, 13, 45, 56, 57, 66, 66-68, 69, 72-73
Nebiolo, *58*
Neufville Digital Futura, 62, 63, *128*, *129*, *170*, *208*
Neurath, Otto, *95*
Neutra, Richard, 178
Neutraface, 178, *180*
Neuzeit Grotesk, 48
New Directions, 42
New Typography (movement), 26, 41
New Yorker, 45
New York Times, 39-40
Nicholas, Robin, *171*
Nike, *129*, *130*, 131, *132*, 132-35, *133*, *134*, 145, 165, 170
Nike 365, 170
Nike 365 Condensed Extra Bold, 170
Nixon, Richard, 13, *73*, 74, *75*
Nobel (typeface), 178
Nolde, Emil, 68
North Vietnam, *103*

Obama, Barack, 74, *77*, 178, *178*
Obey Giant, 144, *145*
One Penn Plaza, New York City, *117*

Pacific Science Center, Seattle, Washington, *136-37*
packaging and labeling, 17, *18*, 95. *See also* Dockers
Papyrus, 14, 19
Paratype Futura, 63, *124*, *125*
Paratype Futura Futuris, *124*, *125*
Party City, *115*
Penrose Annual, 21
Pentagram, 174-75
petrol stations, 122-23
PetSmart, *113*
Photo-Lettering Futura. *See* PL Fute
phototypesetting, 59, 62, 174
PL Fute, *128*, *129*. *See also* Futura Maxi
Poland, 72, 73
political typography, 65-85

INDEX 205

Port Authority Bus Terminal, New York City, *176*, 178
Postal Service Vehicle Maintenance Facility, *119*
Post Office, *119*
Print, 21
Private Property, 121
Proxima Sans, *180*, 181
Public Housing sign, *119*

Queen Elizabeth II Centre, London, England, *110*

Rand, Ann, *41*
 Sparkle and Spin, *41*
Rand, Paul, 24, *41*, 45
 Sparkle and Spin, *41*
 Thoughts on Design, *41*
Rand McNally, *99*
Reagan, Ronald, 74
Reebok, 132
Reichstag (Germany), 66
Renner, Paul, 14, 26–29, 28, 30, 33, 35, 47, *51*, 63, 67, 172, 181
Retina, 169
Rogers, Bruce, 22
Romney, Mitt, *77*, 77
Roscosmos (Russia), *101*
Royal Tenenbaums, The (Anderson), 156–58, *159*, 161
Rubio, Marco, 81, *85*
Rushmore (Anderson), 161
Russia, 101
Russian constructivists, 22
Russian Cyrillic, 35

Samsung, 174
Samsung Sharp Sans, 174
San Francisco, California, 148
sans serif, 20, 34, 39, 41, 47–49, 53, 56, 59, 63, 66, 73, 74, 76, 87, 131, 171, 172, 174, 175, 177–78, 181
Sans Serif (typeface). *See* Kabel
Saturday Evening Post, 44, 45
Saussure, Ferdinand de, 131
Scandal in Paris, A (Sirk), *138*

Scangraphic Futura, *128*, *129*, 208
Schriftguss, 48
Schwartz, Christian, 105, 165, 169, 178
Schwitters, Kurt, *35*
Scott, Ridley,
 The Martian 101
Semplicitá, *58*
Sharp, Lucas, 82, *172*, *174*
Sharp Hartwig Advertising, *136–37*
Sharp Sans, 81, 82, 172, 174, 175
Shell, *123*
Shoppers World, *114*
signage, 104–29
Simonson, Mark, 181
Sirk, Douglas,
 A Scandal in Paris, *138*
Slate, 161
Sleep Number, *108*
Social Democratic Party (Germany), 66, *68*, *76*, *76*
Social Network, The (Fincher), *179*
Sparkle and Spin (Rand, Rand), *41*
Spartan, *48*, *50*, *51*, 56, 59, 62, 63, 73, 78, 79, 88, *150*
SPD. *See* Social Democratic Party (Germany)
Spiekermann, Erik, 47, 165
Steile Futura, *33*
Stempel, 48, *49*
Stephenson Blake, *58*
Stevenson, Adlai E., *75*
Super Grotesk, 48
Supreme (brand), *141*, *141*, *143*, *144*
surrealism, 25
Sutnar, Ladislav, 45, *96*
Sweet's Catalog Service, *96*
Swigert, Jack, 94
Swiss modernism, 22, 41

Tannenburg, *67*
Temple Salon, Frederick, Maryland, *111*
Templin Brink, 148
Tempo, *51*, *53*, *53*, 56, *59*, *59*, 178
Thälmann, Ernst, *69*
Thinking with Type (Lupton), 14
Thompson, Bradbury, 45
Thompson, J. Walter, 164

Thoughts on Design (Rand), 41
Times New Roman, 26, 84–85
Towson Mall parking garage, Towson, Maryland, 116
Trajan, 77, 81, *81*
Trump, Donald, *83*, 84–85
Tschichold, Jan, 33–35, 41, 67
Twentieth Century, *51*, 53, 59, *109*
Type Directors Club, 135
Typography 13, *134*
Typesetters' Book, The (Das Buch des Setzers), 31
Typeshop Futura, *128*, *129*
Typographical Scoreboard, 44

Ukraine, 72, 73
Under Armour, 131
Underground, 56
United Kingdom, 56, 74, *76*, 77
United States, 38–41, 44–45, 48–49, 52, 56, 57, 58–59, 62–63, 73–74, 77, 81, 84, 88–103
United Steel Workers of America, *118*
Unity. *See* Sharp Sans
Universal, 35, *171*
University of Chicago, 15, 21
URW Futura, *124*, *125*
URW No. 2D, *124*, *125*
US Air Force, *102*
US Army, 94–95, *103*, 149
USA Today, *168, 169*, 169–70, *170*
US Office of Civilian Defense, 44
UTOCO highway map, *94*

Valero, *122*
Vampire Weekend albums, *160*
Vanity Fair, 36–37, *38*, 38–40, 41, 44, 52
Verdana, *171*
Vietnam War, *103*
Vignelli, Massimo, 105–6
Vogue, 44–45, 52
Vogue (typeface), 27, *51*, 52, 52–53, *54*, 79
Vogue Berlin, 39
Volkswagen (VW), *162*, 163–65, *164*, *165*, 166–67, 169
Vox, 33
VW. *See* Volkswagen (VW)

VW Copy (typeface), 165, *165*
VW Headline (typeface), 165, *165*, 169

Wagner & Schmidt, 48
Wall Street Journal, 169
Waterstones, Birmingham, England, *110*
Whitney, 81
Why, What, How, Essential Product Information, 96
Wieden+Kennedy, 134
Wolff Olins, 169
World Geographic Atlas: A Composite of Man's Environment, 99
World War I, 48–49
World War II, 44, 45, 58–59, 73, *78*, 95, *102*, 148–49

x-height, 16, 20, 169, *180*

Yefimov, Vladimir, *124*

Zapf, Herman, 19
Zénith, 33

The book is typeset in Commercial Type's Lyon, designed by Kai Bernau. Lyon is a contemporary interpretation of the sixteenth-century French printing and type design of Robert Granjon. The chapter headings are typeset in Neufville Digital's Futura ND Bold.*

*Futura ND Bold is a 1999 interpretation of Futura by Marie-Thérèse Koreman, based on original sources. The captions are typeset in Scangraphic's Futura SB-Medium. All other Futuras used in this book are labled with their respective digital creators. Every Futura has some ancestral link to original sources, but Neufville Digital has a more direct link than most. Neufville Digital was created in 1998 as a collaboration between Bauer Type in Barcelona and Visualogik Technology & Design in the Netherlands. Bauer Types, SL, is the legal successor to the original Bauer Type Foundry (Bauersche Giesserei) that first issued Futura in 1927. As such Neufville Digital has access to many of Paul Renner's original drawings and Bauer Type Foundry's early test prints. The name Futura is not unique to Neufville Digital, in spite of its legal pedigree, because the name was licensed by Bauer to many other type companies in the early years of digitization. All manufacturers who use the name Futura license the name from Bauer and Renner's family.